ESCAPE

A Sequel to *Terror by Night and Day*

Marie Abelian Egitkhanoff
with Ken Wilson

Pacific Press Publishing Association
Mountain View, California
Oshawa, Ontario

Cover illustration by Tim Mitoma

Library of Congress Cataloging in Publication Data

Egitkhanoff, Marie Abelian.
Escape.

Summary: Relates the further struggles of a young Armenian girl and her people who have temporarily settled in Konya, a city in central Turkey.
1. Egitkhanoff, Marie Abelian. 2. Armenians—Turkey—Biography. 3. Armenian massacres, 1915-1923. [1. Egitkhanoff, Marie Abelian. 2. Armenians—Turkey—Biography. 3. Armenian massacres, 1915-1923] I. Wilson, Ken. II. Title.
DS195.5.E378 956.1'00491992 [92] 81-10526
ISBN 0-8163-0439-4 AACR2

CONTENTS

Synopsis 7
Losing Our Tracks 10
"Bread Shall Be Given" 17
Cat-and-Mouse Game in Konya 21
Days of Uncertainty 31
Unlucky Baron Lucky 41
Baron Lucky Again 47
Countdown to "I Do" 55
An Unusual Ceremony 69
Good News 75
The Waiting Game 82
The Return 87
Uneasy Peace 95
"Confusion and Every Evil Work" 103
The Storm Breaks 107
A New Life 114
Land of Promise 121

Synopsis of
Terror by Night and Day

"A thousand shall fall at thy side, and ten thousand at thy right hand; but it shall not come nigh thee." Psalm 91:7.

This promise we saw literally fulfilled when we survived and then escaped from the "death march" involving the Armenian people in Turkey during World War I. My mother, my sister Heripsime with her four children, and I were miraculously plucked from the exile herd by a kindhearted Turkish officer before we reached the dreaded Syrian Desert—and oblivion. In this "death march" more than half a million Armenian people in Turkey perished by various means—starvation, disease, exhaustion, actual massacre.

We had left my sister's home in Shak-shak, a village near Yalova on the eastern shore of the Sea of Marmara, on August 15, 1915. With our few portable belongings transported on a hired ox cart, we walked the many weary miles through Iznik (ancient Nicea) to the railroad on the Sakarya River. Along the way my mother had her foot crushed under the wheel of the ox cart. This injury, without the benefit of medical care, caused her untold misery and left her crippled for the rest of her life.

Because we had money to pay our fare, we were permitted to travel by rail—crammed like sardines in filthy cattle cars. At Eskisehir we visited briefly with my oldest sister, Varsenig Pirenian—she outside the car, we on the inside looking out through the open slats. Varsenig was never sent into exile, because her husband was an officer in the Turkish army and because she was associated with a Protestant mission in the city. Turkish officials in different areas enforced the eviction orders according to their own whims.

After enduring extreme hardships and after a long encampment near Afyon, we were forced into a "cattle-car pullman" again and sent off toward the Syrian plains. (Several times at Afyon we had avoided evacuation by quickly moving our camp away from the area being cleared.)

At Eregli in the extreme southeastern corner of Anatolia, just north of the Taurus Mountains, we were herded off the train and into another detention camp. We understood that from this point on everyone must walk—regardless of physical condition—across the mountain pass and on toward the Syrian Desert. And we knew that literally thousands of exiles had died along the way from starvation, exhaustion, disease, brutality, or sheer massacre.

Our little family group of seven had managed to stay together despite brutal efforts to drive loved ones apart. Mother and I felt bound by honor—Heripsime's husband, Lazarus, also a soldier, had charged us solemnly to stay with his family. But now, after a night of agony and prayer, I determined that I would not go any farther despite Heripsime's desire to stay with her husband's people from Shak-shak.

Providentially, the regular officer in charge of the detention camp had been sent somewhere else for a month or so. The temporary commander proved to be a kind provincial governor who, we later learned, had allowed many exiles to go to his city instead of walking ahead to almost certain death. This gentleman listened sympathetically to my pleas and pitied Mother's crippled condition. He sent us with two other families to the isolated city of Sultaniye (Karapinar). At the last moment Heripsime decided to go with Mother and me.

A rigorous winter and a sweltering summer in this "graveyard of the living dead" (as I named the place) reduced us to emaciated and malaria-ridden derelicts. Unbelievable hardships and terrifying experiences made us fear that we could not survive much longer. Then another miracle delivered us.

A group of important Russian prisoners of war (treated more like guests of the government) had arrived in Sultaniye during the winter. Among them was a young Armenian, disguised as a Russian officer serving as interpreter between the Russians and the Turks. Yagof (Jacob) Egitkhanoff, whom we nicknamed Baron Lucky or Lucky Boy, soon developed an interest in me and my Sabbath-keeping religion. He made connections and worked out arrangements for Mother and me to escape from Sultaniye to Konya (ancient Iconium) in the fall of 1916.

In Konya we hoped to find safe lodging among the Armenian residents of the city. Because Konya is a sacred city to Turkish Muslims, and because the religious leaders there ignored the government's order to deport all Armenians, a large section of the city remained a safe haven for those fortunate inhabitants. However, the authorities tried to ferret out escaped exiles who posed as residents.

The book *Terror by Night and Day* ends with our arrival at the inn where the "underground railway" delivered escaping exiles.

Losing Our Tracks

Two weary exiles now free in a strange city! Free? Yes, Mother and I had escaped from the "graveyard of the living dead," as we called the miserable little town of Sultaniye. But we were far from being safe.

"Have a good rest for a few hours," the innkeeper told us, "but first thing in the morning you must lose your tracks in the city."

The young men carried our baggage up the stairs to a room on the mezzanine. "It would be very easy for you to fall into the hands of enemies," one of them told us. "The Turkish authorities frequently search this place to find runaway exiles. You must quickly find someone in the city who knows you and who will help you blend in with the Armenian residents of the city." Then they left us alone to get some sleep.

With the dawn the boys came to awaken us. But we had not slept a wink because of the intense emotions that gripped us. The joy of deliverance from past dangers and hardship alternated with apprehension for present and future hazards. We were both weak from the ravages of malaria and from the strain of the journey just ended. But we had to leave the inn at once.

We would have to find a place to stay. We knew of

several Armenian families who should be able to help us. But how would we buy food? We would need a *vesika*—a ration paper. But the *vesika* would be issued only to registered inhabitants. How could we register without explaining our situation as newcomers? We really needed help.

First we decided that we would find Mrs. Hovivian, the wife of the Protestant pastor we had met in Sultaniye. She would be near the Protestant church, we were certain. Her two older daughters worked for an American institution there, and the Americans had arranged for Mrs. Hovivian and two younger daughters to be released from Sultaniye. (The pastor had died from beatings and torture he suffered after his attempt to escape and join his wife.) We felt sure that Mrs. Hovivian would be able to advise us.

In answer to our knock, she opened her door. Seeing us standing there, she clapped her hand over her mouth and stood in silent amazement for a moment. Then she began to weep. "Oh, Ebross Abelian and Mary!" she exclaimed between sobs. "Come in! Come in!"

"No," Mother said firmly, "we must not. We must quickly find relatives or friends where we can stay before the authorities catch us. We ran away."

This touched off a new round of weeping. "You sheltered my husband during his attempt to escape. He died, but you made it." Memories of the bitter experiences made it impossible for her to contain her emotions.

"Can you tell us where to go?" I asked gently. "We must find a place today."

"Yes, yes." Mrs. Hovivian controlled her weeping. "Ebross, your daughter's husband's brother, Gabriel Pirenian, is living here in Konya. A few weeks ago he and his family moved from the Armenian quarter into a Turkish section of the city near the Yeshil Tubré

Djamie Mosque. I hope he is still there after the recent city-wide sweep to round up illegal Armenian residents."

She went on to explain that Gabriel and his family had somehow managed to establish themselves as legal residents and had secured *vesikas*. They had moved to the part of town near the mosque, the prestigious center of the Dede Muslim holy men, to make it easier to escape detection by the authorities.

Mrs. Hovivian asked a young Turkish boy to guide us to the address she gave. Even in this simple walk through town we had to be careful. The boy would go along one side of the street, and we would follow at a distance on the other side. Also we tried to keep curious eyes from seeing our emaciated faces. I was dressed as an old woman in a dark print dress, and of course, I had to walk slowly with Mother as she limped along.

The boy led us along a street that skirted the mosque. He cut through a corner of the mosque grounds and headed into the Turkish section of town. He passed several cross streets and then turned onto the street where we were supposed to find the Pirenians.

We had not gone far along that street before we noticed a man ahead of us carrying a load of household articles on his back. By this time Mother was quite tired of walking—and so was I, to be quite truthful—but it seemed as if something impelled us to overtake that man. It was almost as if a strong wind drove us along. Soon we came up beside the man, and Mother caught a glimpse of his face. She turned to me and whispered, "Isn't that Papa Paul?" I looked, and it was. We were momentarily speechless.

At about the same instant the man stopped and looked full into Mother's face. "Oh, Sister Ebross, is it you?" he exclaimed. He was so excited at seeing us that he almost dropped his load. "I thought you were dead!" he blurted. "What are you doing up here in Konya?" Since the deportation we had not seen one another nor heard any report. Papa Paul could hardly contain his emotions.

Quietly Mother explained about our presence. We knew that we must be careful not to attract attention. "We are trying to find Gabriel Pirenian," she said. "We must find a place to stay before dark."

Our young guide saw that we had stopped, so he waited farther along on the other side of the street. We motioned for him to come back. We gave him baksheesh (money), and he left us to return to his home.

"I'll take you to Gabriel's place as soon as I get this load off my back," Papa Paul said. He told us that he and his family were moving into the Turkish section to escape close scrutiny by the authorities. They had rented the guesthouse in a fine Turkish home. "Ebross *Koir* (Dear friend Ebross)," he said, "you can stay with us. You are welcome! My wife would like to have you with us." He couldn't stop marveling about our providential meeting on the street.

We entered through a large high gate into the familiar Turkish guesthouse arrangement—animals (donkeys, horses, or camels) used the same entrance to reach the *develig*, or stable, just beyond and adjoining the guest room. This room had the familiar *sedirlik*—a built-up earthen bench along one wall. It was much like the rooms we had occupied in Sultaniye, with one major difference—in this one the dirt floor and halfway up the walls were wet. One could not be too choosey in that crowded city, so long as one could have a roof overhead and walls for privacy. We needed a place for the night, and here was one offered to us. We had to be thankful for this providence.

Papa Paul deposited his load in the room and told us that he would show us where Gabriel Pirenian lived. Then he would go on for another load. His wife and his daughter would be with him when he returned. We followed him to the place he said the Pirenians lived.

Mother and I entered the gate which opened into an enclosed yard where a number of Armenian children played. As soon as they knew we were looking for the Pirenians, they called out the names of Gabriel's children.

Two of the Pirenian children dashed out of the upstairs apartment onto a small porch and looked down. "Oh, Ebross *Koir*!" they shouted. "And Mary!"

At once the porch filled as two other children and their parents spilled through the door. They stood there like statues, unable to believe their eyes.

"Is it really you? Where did you come from? How did you get here?" The questions tumbled over one another.

We climbed the stairs as quickly as possible and quieted them down. "Silence, friends! Silence, please!" Mother commanded. "We ran away. Let no one know about this. The children must also be very careful not to tell anyone."

Briefly we told these dear ones of our escape from the "graveyard of the living dead." Of course we were happy for our deliverance, but our joy could not be full until my sister Heripsime and her children could join us. We must somehow find a way to bring them to Konya.

After a short visit with Gabriel's family we returned to the place that the Boghosians had rented. We had to be off the streets long before dark.

How grateful we were for the hospitality of the Boghosians, Papa Paul and Mother Makrouhi. They willingly made room in their small place for two half-dead fugitives. Fortunately they had not told the Turkish landlords how many people would be moving in; therefore our addition to the family was not noticed as it would have been if we had arrived even one day later.

Papa Paul and Mother Makrouhi had a mattress of corn husks on the dirt floor in one corner of the room. Mother and I shared a pad stuffed with wool on the floor in another corner (we slept head-to-foot under the same cover). Takouhy (Queenie), the teenaged daughter, had a narrow pad on one end of the *sedirlik*; and Dikran Mazloumian, Mother Makrouhi's nephew, slept on the other end.

That first night nobody slept very much. There was too much to talk about. Quiet conversation, low laughter, and subdued sobbing flowed on until well past midnight. Then sheer exhaustion closed our eyes in merciful sleep.

With the new day came the pressing realization that we must somehow obtain a *visika* for bread. The Boghosians had three; but now there were three fugitives, Mother, myself, and Dikran, in the house without ration tickets. The amount of bread allowed for one ticket would barely supply enough for one person. Obviously six people could not subsist very long on three rations. Other food was fairly plentiful, but bread was essential for a balanced diet.

Dikran Mazloumian had escaped the "bachelors' death march" when the train he had been put on reached Konya. He was sure he could find relatives or friends in the city where he could stay, and he had found his aunt. Actually Dikran was married and had a family, but officers had arrested him on the streets of Istanbul as a bachelor. They had sent him off into exile without bothering to check his claim that he was engaged in legitimate work—not a deserter from the army. (By law all able-bodied unmarried men were to be in the military service or other approved labor.) Another interesting connection was the fact the Dikran was Gabriel's cousin; Mother Makrouhi was an aunt to both of them.

What could we do? Always hanging over us like a black cloud was the fear of recognition—of being captured as fugitives. Often news made its way through the Armenian homes that so-and-so had been arrested and sent back on the death march. I was told that if the authorities arrested me, they would tie me to a horse's tail and drag me back to Sultaniye—the "graveyard of the living dead."

Over and over God's comforting promise sounded in my ears: "Fear thou not; for I am with thee: be not dismayed; for I am thy God: I will strengthen thee; yea, I will help thee; yea, I will uphold thee with the right hand of my righteousness." Isaiah 41:10.

“‘Bread Shall Be Given’”

The promise of Isaiah 33:16 is that to the one who walketh righteously his “bread shall be given him.” We often repeat the Lord’s prayer without really thinking what the words mean: “Give us this day our daily bread.” Of course that request includes the Bread of Life—spiritual nourishment—but we exiles in Konya needed physical bread. How were we to get it?

Not many days after Mother and I moved in with the Boghosians, two kindhearted sisters, Christine and Nevart Azarian, came to visit us. They had also escaped from Sultaniye but before we did. They had somehow secured *vesikas* for bread, and they had thought of a plan.

“Ebross *Meirig* (Mother Ebross),” said Christine, “we can get bread for you. We are not going to let you starve here.”

They showed us their tickets. “See.” Nevart pointed to the ticket. “At the bakery they make a check mark with pencil for the ration received on that day. All we will have to do is erase the mark, go to a different bakery, and get a second ration.”

“No!” Mother said. “That is not right.”

“Yes, it will be right,” Christine said. The sisters stood up to leave. “Listen. You will be buying the bread with your own money. That is not stealing."

"We are not going to let you starve," Nevart said, repeating her sister's earlier declaration. "You are half dead already. You must eat to regain your health."

And so we had bread—at least for the time being. But both Mother and I felt uneasy about this illegal means of getting food. We knew that the danger of detection was real. It seemed that wherever we turned, we had to do something wrong in order to survive.

Then a dramatic turn of events proved again the Bible promise, that "God shall supply all your need."

One day Takouhy and I decided to do some house cleaning. We started by washing the window. The one large window in the room opened into a narrow passageway between the guesthouse and a high mud-brick wall. As we worked, we chatted about our experiences since the deportation, laughing about the humorous and talking soberly about the tragic—as any two young women would. Suddenly we noticed a strangely dressed man at the corner of the house just inside the passageway. He seemed to be listening intently to our conversation. When he saw that we had discovered him, he stood motionless for a moment, then turned and slipped noiselessly out the gate, securing the latch as the gate closed.

We had not heard anyone enter the gate, and we had no idea how long the man had been there. We had never seen him before, so we did not know who he was. One fact gave us some consolation: he wore the distinctive clothing of a Kurd tribesman. We concluded, therefore, that he could not have understood our conversation in the Armenian tongue.

Many Kurds, nomadic tribesmen, from the northeastern part of Turkey had been moved from the Russian and Iranian border areas into central Turkey. They came with their tents and their animals, and hundreds of them were now camped in the fields outside Konya. The townspeople resented and feared these nomads; many stories circulated about cruelty and atrocities perpetrated by the strangers. One story supposedly founded on fact claimed that a Kurd tribesman had captured, killed, baked, and eaten an Armenian child.

In the evening following the eavesdropping episode, soon after dark, an Armenian friend came to our house. For a long time the woman talked with Mother Makrouhi in the hall. Finally Takouhy and I went out to see what was going on. We found out that this woman, Nunufar Shakerjian, had learned a great deal about Mother and me.

The Kurd had gone immediately and told *Digin* (Mrs.) Shakerjian everything he had heard. Actually he was not a Kurd but an Armenian youth named Ampartzoum. However, he dressed like a Kurd and used a Moslem name, Mehmed. We learned that this young man was a trusted servant in the household of the Kurd commander in the Konya area. Actually, Mehmed had been appointed overseer of bread distribution among the Kurds. Nobody outside the commander's household knew of Mehmed's Armenian connection except the Shakerjians, and they were careful not to tell. *Digin* Shakerjian told us now that she and Mehmed were going to figure out how to provide bread for us.

Two evenings later *Digin* Nunufar Shakerjian, her face lighted with a smile, came to see us. "Here are two loaves of bread Mehmed brought for you," she said. "He had arranged to get bread for us. He may be able to do this every day, or at least as often as you need it until you can find a better way."

Oh, how gratitude overwhelmed us. Words could not express our thankfulness. Just to think—the young man who had sneaked in to eavesdrop on our conversation was now providing us with bread.

Konya bread, made of whole wheat flour, had wonderful flavor and high nutritional value. It was nothing like the tough, gritty bread supplied to us in the exile camps. With better food and a change in climate, Mother and I began to regain our strength. Our malaria attacks subsided, and our faces filled out again. A healthy pink replaced the paleness that had marked us as exiles. The water, good and pure, we could drink without fear of it being polluted. How we praised the Lord for fulfilling His promise of bread and water.

We also enjoyed many pleasant hours spent in the lovely yard of the big house. The Turkish landlord, a very refined gentleman, and his young wife told us to spend time in their yard whenever we liked. There, surrounded by fruit trees, flowers, and a vegetable garden, we passed many happy hours.

Takouhy took care of the little Turkish boy, a toddler, much of the time. The Boghosians and Mother and I paid our rent by doing various kinds of work for the Turkish family. Our mothers spun wool yarn, and we girls knitted all kinds of warm garments. Often we girls would help with the housework, even assisting in serving meals for guests occasionally.

Life seemed to be settling into a more pleasant routine.

Cat-and-Mouse Game in Konya

Then news came. Some bringing joy, but more causing deep grief, came to us through the Armenian grapevine. Our hearts yearned for information about our friends and relatives in exile.

Several weeks after our arrival in Konya we learned that my sister Heripsime and her children had arranged with authorities to leave Sultaniye. She had come to Konya and had rented quarters on the other side of the city near her husband's people from Shak-shak. Great joy filled our hearts to know that my sister was safe. Others who had shared our misery in that "graveyard of the living dead" had also managed to make their way to Konya.

Most news, however, carried a somber tone. The list of casualties seemed endless. It was at this time we learned of my cousin Varham Abelian's death under the heartless boots of gendarmes when they cut down the tent on his fever-wracked body.

Lazarus, Heripsime's husband had been released from military service and sent to Syria on the pretext that he could search for his family. Instead of being allowed to go where he wanted, he was driven along in the death march until he starved to death. He, with thousands of others, tried to prolong life by searching the fields for roots or edible herbs, only to expire after many days of declining vitality. The Armenians had a current saying: "Those who fall by the sword are counted more fortunate than those who starve."

Frightening news began to sweep through Konya. Military recruiters renewed their efforts to round up all able-bodied Armenians on the pretext of putting them in the army. But we all knew that most men thus inducted found themselves headed for sure death in the Syrian desert—the inescapable slaughterhouse. Officers apprehended men on the streets; therefore, men of likely age began hiding inside houses. Officers, aware of this ruse, often invaded homes without warning to look for men.

Armenian families living in Turkish guesthouses had an advantage at this time. Officers could not enter a Turkish yard without first giving Muslim women time to seclude themselves. This interval gave opportunity for any Armenian man on the premises to hide. The Armenian women used all kinds of ruses to conceal their men; one effective method was to roll the man inside bedding and drag the roll into a closet. The searchers then would see only a pile of bedding.

Since we did not have an unlimited supply of money, it was necessary for us to find some source of income. Mother, crippled as she was, went to work with Papa Paul pruning in the vineyards. Some of our younger men, including Gabriel Pirenian and Dikran Mazloumian, secured employment making charcoal in the mountains for a Turkish *pasha* (high-ranking official). This saved them from the military roundup for a time, and they could arrange their own work schedule so as to keep the Sabbath.

I knew that I must also find employment as soon as I regained strength. I had hoped to go to work in the American hospital, but this could not be arranged.

However, through the interest of Elder Frauchiger of the International Tract Society in Istanbul (the man who had tried to arrange my release from Sultaniye), I was introduced to *Schwester* (Sister) Clara, a German nun. This woman supervised the kitchen at the German *Soldatenheim* (Soldier's Home). The task here was to provide meals for companies of German soldiers passing through Konya on their way to fight the British in Egypt or Mesopotamia.

I was soon caught up in the swirl of activity—my job, peeling endless quantities of boiled potatoes and then helping to wait on the tables. Best of all, Sister Clara told me to eat all the potatoes I wanted. What a blessed treat. If I could only work there forever!

But that evening, instead of sending me home with another woman, Sister Clara took me to the mansion home of Herr Mauer, the chief of the railroad. The spacious three-story building dominated the residential area near the railroad station. Herr Mauer lived with his mother, but he spent most of his time traveling on business for the railroad. Frau Mauer was a highly temperamental woman—thoroughly spoiled. Nothing, it seemed, could please her. Oddly, she took a liking to me when Herr Mauer introduced us. I say oddly, because she had an implacable hatred for Armenians.

Sister Clara explained to me, after we left the Mauer mansion and walked toward my home, that it would be better for me to stay in that home and be a companion to Frau Mauer than to work in the Soldatenheim, where hundreds of young soldiers stopped. She thought that it was not proper or safe for a young woman to expose herself to that rough and unprincipled element.

I appreciated the personal concern of this kind-hearted nun; so the next day I returned to the Mauer residence.

Frau Mauer asked me if I could work for her each day and then return to my home each evening. She had two reasons for this request: one obviously to try me out for a few days; the other to work out a solution for my sleeping quarters. The house had a large finished attic with a furnished room in one end. The problem was that Herr Mauer's fiancée, a German nurse named Elsie, temporarily occupied that room. Elsie would be moving out in a few days, Frau Mauer informed me.

I could not safely walk the streets alone, especially in the early morning or late afternoon of the short days of late autumn; so I had to find someone to accompany me. For that purpose I arranged with Tadeus, a boy whom we had known in Sultaniye and who now lived in Konya, to make the trip with me twice a day. It was a long walk from one side of town to the other.

One evening as Tadeus and I passed near the courthouse in the center of town, we noticed three men we immediately recognized as officials from Sultaniye. One of them was none other than the persistant post-master I had had trouble with when we had lived in Sultaniye. I had nicknamed him The Tiger because of his determined efforts to make me his prey.

I was terrified!

As the three men approached, I distinctly heard one of the men say in a loud voice, "That's the very person you are looking for!" He pointed to me.

"Oh, it couldn't be," said the second man. Then after a pause, "She does resemble the girl though."

I could immediately tell that they were not sure. I now wore good clothes, and I walked with a healthy spring in my step. No, they did not know for sure, but I knew they would try to find out.

The Tiger called out, "Why did you run away and come here?"

Without a word I turned into a side street and hurried off in another direction. Tadeus had presence of mind enough to cross the street and continue along the other side. We both pretended that we had not heard anything. I slipped from sight around another corner before the three men could see where I had gone. Soon Tadeus joined me, and we hurried on to the safety of my home—the crowded guesthouse in a Turkish compound.

Mother had worried before about my walking in the streets. Now she said, "Sooner or later they will catch you somewhere, my child. You'd better stop!" To be truthful, my own fears increased also.

The next morning poor old Papa Paul made the long trip with me—a real sacrifice for him.

Providentially, Frau Mauer told me that Fräulein Elsie had vacated the room; now I could stay there. What a luxury compared to the cramped quarters in the one-room guesthouse. Here I had a comfortable bed with a pigeon-down quilt; there I slept head-to-foot with Mother on a thin wool pad spread on the damp floor, and we shared a worn quilt.

But I couldn't be happy. All night long, it seemed, my mind relived the miseries I had seen and endured. I could not erase those vivid pictures—pleading eyes in faces made gaunt by hunger, shivering bodies poorly clad against the bitter cold, bleeding feet from walking shoeless over miles of rocky roads, parched lips and swollen tongues because of endless hours under a scorching sun without a sip of water. I thought over and over of my dear mother and wished she could share my comfort now as she had shared my hardships for the more than two years of exile. I ventured one day to suggest to Frau Mauer that my mother might stay with me. The woman would not listen to such an idea. She hated all Armenians—except me—and would not even think of allowing another one in her home.

Frau Mauer never could understand why I refused to eat food prepared with pork or rabbit, and she never ceased trying to persuade me to eat it. "You are so undernourished," she would declare. "You should not fuss about food. You need to gain weight and look pretty."

When I tried to show her from her German Bible that God cares what we eat and drink, she would snort. "Oh, nonsense! That was all in the past—for the Jews. Forget about such things!"

Keeping the seventh-day Sabbath raised another issue, but on this point the eccentric old lady did not oppose me. I pointed out that "the seventh day is the sabbath of the Lord thy God" and that I was observing His command to "remember the sabbath day, to keep it holy."

"Mary, I love you so much," Frau Mauer declared, "that I will let Ahmed Agha walk with you to the place where your Sabbath friends meet."

Ahmed, a kind Turkish soldier, had the unmilitary job of taking care of Frau Mauer's yard and the animals. He proved to be a gentle and understanding friend. Whenever Frau Mauer felt well enough to be left alone for a few hours and when she felt in a good mood, Ahmed Agha walked with me to church.

Frau Mauer frequently stated her determination to take me with her to Germany. She would adopt me and find a good husband for me, she declared. She tried to induce me to make friends with one and another of the young German officers who frequently came to dinner. And, of course, she couldn't understand why I would not join in their drinking parties. Although she usually scoffed at my strict principles and ridiculed my defense based on scriptural teaching, she repeatedly asked me to read the texts from her German Bible. I thoroughly enjoyed these occasions.

Meanwhile Gabriel Pirenian, Dikran Mazloumian, and the others returned to Konya from their job of making charcoal in the mountains. We all thought that it would be best for Dikran to find a job, as I had done, among the Germans. So I asked the man in charge of the *Soldatenheim* if he could give Dikran some kind of work. The Germans put Dikran to work in the kitchen under the supervision of Sister Clara. Several other Armenian men worked there already—men who had been pastors of small Protestant churches in various places. Now Dikran did not have to hide in his aunt's house in constant fear of being discovered by raiding Turkish officials. We all thought he would be comparatively safe here.

One day Dikran was sent to help transport some crates from the railroad to the *Soldatenheim*. Turkish officers suddenly appeared and arrested the young man as a deserter from the army. They pushed him into a train car where other arrested men had been locked up.

News of the arrest shocked all of us. I felt personally guilty because it was my arrangements that had secured this job for him, thinking in this job he would be safe.

As soon as I learned of the arrest, I asked for permission to take some of Dikran's personal belongings to the railroad. I found an older Armenian woman who gladly accompanied me. We went to the *Soldatenheim* and asked Sister Clara for Dikran's Bible and a bundle of clothing. She also gave us a little money to give him.

The next day my mother and Mother Makrouhi Boghosian (Dikran's aunt) went to the railroad to visit him, but the train had pulled out. How sad we all felt!

Jesus promises that "sorrow shall be turned into joy." John 16:20. In this case the promise was speedily fulfilled. It was not long before a letter came from Istanbul. A letter from Dikran. He told how his arrest had turned out to be a blessing. The train stopped at a place called Ouzoun Keoprou. Somehow he had managed to escape from the train and had made his way to Istanbul and his family. The rest of the "soldiers" were sent away on the death march "to find their families"—only to perish as had thousands of others. Dikran wrote a few lines to me personally. He knew that I had taken the blame for his arrest, and he wanted to reassure me that it had turned out to be a blessing.

The late autumn of 1916 brought unusually cold weather to central Turkey. Much suffering resulted. It should have been no problem to me—living as I was in a fine home. My room had a small heater, for which Ahmed brought up kindling and coal. But when Frau Mauer was in a bad mood, she would not allow him or me to start a fire. She also slept in an attic room adjoining mine. The difference was that her room opened on a stairway through which heat came from the rest of the house, and she insisted that I must keep my door closed. As a result of this arrangement my room became a veritable refrigerator. I would work in the warm kitchen or other parts of the house all day. At bedtime I would carry a copper bed warmer filled with hot water to Frau Mauer's room. I would do all I could to make her comfortable. Then I would retire to my ice-cold room and be chilled to the bone by the time I crawled under the covers. I could not understand the woman—her frequent protestations of love for me and her adamant refusal to allow a fire in my heater or at least permission to leave my door open for a bit of warmth from the rest of the house.

One particularly cold night I couldn't stop shivering when I got into bed. The next morning I awoke with chills and fever. The malaria, which had not bothered me since the day we escaped from Sultaniye, came back with a vengeance. I was so sick that I could not get up. Fortunately for me, Elsie had spent the night at the house, so she took care of me.

Elsie's tender care for me made Frau Mauer jealous, and she became very angry. At first she vented her anger on Elsie. Finally she came to my room, but to me she was gentle and sweet. She told me that she thought it would be best for me to go and be with my own people until I recovered. That idea suited me well.

Frau Mauer called for Ahmed Agha and told him to accompany me to the Boghosian's house, where my mother lived. After saying, "*Auf wiedersehen*," we set out across town. Because of my weak condition we rode a streetcar as far as possible, but there was still quite a distance to walk through the Yeshil Tubré Djamie Mosque grounds and on to the street where the Turkish house stood.

"I hope you will soon recover and return to work for the old lady," Ahmed said as he turned to go back. "I will then have the joy of walking with you again on Sabbath when you go to worship with the others. We all have to be patient," he said. "Take care of yourself, young lady." And the gracious Turk left me at the gate.

Here I was—back in the crowded one-room guesthouse with its damp walls and wet floor. But I could not complain. This shelter among kind friends was our home in exile. I was glad to be back with Mother and the Boghosians, and they welcomed me wholeheartedly.

One cold early morning in December Takouhy and I had to stand in line instead of our mothers for the Boghosian's bread. After a long wait we received the bread and started home. Suddenly I noticed three

Turkish officers coming toward us, and I recognized one of them. He had been on duty in Sultaniye at the time Mother and I had escaped. From the motions he made with his hands as he spoke to the others, I felt sure he recognized me. I knew that if they got hold of me, they would send me back to die, as had happened to hundreds of other exiles.

Takouhy had not sensed the danger. She had legal papers assuring her of her right to be in Konya. I had no papers. For a moment panic seized me. Then I whispered, "Oh, Takouhy, I am in danger. Let us cross the street. Don't talk. We must slip away quickly and find another way home."

We crossed the street and turned into a side street. The three officers quickened their pace and followed us. We turned one corner after another until we finally lost sight of our pursuers momentarily. At that moment we spied a narrow passage between two walls. We slipped into this space and found a little niche that sheltered us from sight. There we stood, hardly daring to breathe. Voices and hurried footsteps from the street soon told us that the three men had passed our hiding place. Finally we ventured out cautiously and peered along the street in both directions. All appeared clear. Fearful at every corner that we might encounter our enemies, we made our way home.

Days of Uncertainty

Rumors from the outside world penetrated into central Turkey. Nobody could be sure what was going on. It seemed that threatened disaster from Russian armies had disappeared, but on other fronts the news carried ominous portents. British forces were preparing for a new assault on the Tigris-Euphrates valley from the Persian Gulf. German armies were bogged down in their drive toward Paris. We also heard that a British officer named Lawrence was inciting the Arabian tribes in the desert to revolt against Turkish control. The outlook appeared exceedingly gloomy for the German-Turkish coalition. Such conditions forced Turkish authorities to step up the drive of recruiting men for military service.

The new governor of the province of Konya in 1917 ordered a systematic search for deserters and illegal residents. Under such circumstances it was hazardous for Mother or me to be on the street at any time. But in order to live we had to carry on some business. The angel of the Lord surely encamped about us and spared our lives many times.

One day I found it necessary to walk across town. Another girl accompanied me. Suddenly we noticed several Turkish gentlemen approaching. Fear gripped me as I saw that they were watching me closely. Several factors immediately affected me. As I looked toward the men, bright sunlight irritated my eyes so that they crossed and tears began to run. The new shoes I wore hurt my feet so that I limped. When the men came nearer, one of them said, "Poor thing. She is not the one you are looking for. She is both blind and lame." So they felt sorry for me and passed on. How happy I was that the men were Muslims, and Muslims feel it a religious duty to show compassion toward the physically or mentally handicapped.

Word came through the grapevine that a member of an Armenian family from Ankara wanted to see me. A young man had miraculously made his way back from the desert massacres of Deir-e-Zor and had stopped en route at Sultaniye. There he had stayed at the same inn where certain Russian captives were housed. The captive had asked the young man to deliver some letters and a small package to me in Konya. Of course, I knew at once that Russian captive must be Yagof Egitkhanoff.

One of the older Armenian women set out with me to find the address on Atesh Oglou Street. We were told to ask for "Kestenedjilen." After a long search we found the place, and a young gentleman came out of hiding to meet us. He gave me two letters from Onnig Pirenian, my brother-in-law, in Jerusalem; and a small package from Yagof.

In my excitement I hardly knew which to open first. My curiosity impelled me to open the package. It contained fresh butter for Mother and me.

The letters from Onnig told more details about the death of Lazarus, Heripsime's husband, and other sad news. My tears cast a sober spell over the others, and we shared our sorrow over the tragedies that were so common. The young man told of some of the unbelievable butcheries he had witnessed and escaped. After a short visit with these people we took our leave. I thanked the young man for his kindness and gave the family a small portion of the sweet butter Yagof had sent to me.

One day I went to the *Soldatenheim* to see Sister Clara and found her ill in bed. She asked me to sit by her bed so she could talk with me.

"The news is very bad, Mary dear," she said. "Many Germans must return home because of the critical situation." She sighed deeply. "Even Herr Mauer may have to leave and go to the field with the army. He thinks he may have to leave on March 18. He is sick and in the hospital now, and another German officer has already come to take charge of the railroads."

Yes, the ills of the world looked dismal indeed; but of much more immediate concern to me and my mother was the need for bread. My Turkish friend, Agha, was able to buy two loaves of bread for me from the bakery near the depot. As a Turkish man he had no difficulty; but it would have been a disaster for me to attempt such a purchase—I had no *vesika*, and I had no resident papers. I would have been arrested on the spot.

So, although two loaves of bread brought temporary relief, our problem was far from being solved. The bread through the Kurdish source never was sufficient, and various conditions made this supply sporadic. Also we had to buy other food. Mother and I used all kinds of methods for obtaining food so that we would not have to accept help from the Boghosians' scant supplies. One of Heripsime's friends from Shak-shak urged us to petition the government for aid because Lazarus, Heripsime's husband had died as a soldier in official service, although actually he had starved while searching in vain for his family among the exiles. But Gabriel warned us that to file a petition might disclose our status as escaped exiles.

Finally the need for food became so critical that Heripsime filed a petition for herself and her children and included Mother. When the authorities considered the petition, they granted aid for Heripsime and her children; but they ruled that Mother was not part of the family and thus was not eligible. Fortunately, Mother's status as an escapee did not come to notice. Now Mother and I still had no immediate relief; we simply had to trust that the Lord would provide—and He did. A little money came through the Protestant mission from the Near East Relief, and Mother went with Papa Paul to prune someone's vineyard once in a while. Also occasionally Takouhy and I helped our landlady serve dinner for her husband's guests. Always, in every spare moment and when our health permitted, we worked at spinning yarn and knitting or crocheting it into bootees, sweaters, and other articles for sale.

Meanwhile rumors rustled through the Armenian community like dry leaves scattered by the cold February wind. New officials in the Turkish government were supposed to be viewing the Armenian situation from more favorable angles. Armenian soldiers, it was reported, had been praised for their bravery. The surviving exiles would soon be returned to their homes—this promise was supposed to have been made to the American ambassador. Each repatriated exile would receive ten gold liras, the rumor stated.

As if to provide some confirmation to the rumors, a train with eight carloads of Armenian orphans stopped in Konya. These children, gathered from the vicinity of Aleppo and Hama, were en route to Istanbul.

Mother and I, with Mother Makrouhi and a younger woman, went to the railroad station to see if we could find any of our relatives among the orphans. For six hours we stood in the cold, vainly looking for a recognizable face. The only result of our anxious search was that my old enemy, malaria, returned.

Our problem of obtaining bread was no nearer to solution than it had been months before when we arrived in Konya. We still had no *vesika*, and we were in constant danger of being recognized as escaped exiles. The various means we had used for buying bread—when we were fortunate enough to have money—gave only temporary relief.

One day the Azarian sisters came to see us again. They understood our situation, and again they urged us to use their *vesika* to buy some bread, but we were afraid to try. The conversation, as usual, quickly turned to the horrors of the exile; and the sisters could not be comforted for the loss of their two brothers who had died of fever in Sultaniye.

I read to them some of the promises from my Armenian Bible, trying to bring the hope of life with Jesus beyond the sorrows of this mortal life.

For some reason the Azarian sisters brought up the subject of the seventh-day Sabbath. Why, they questioned, had the Roman Church changed the day of worship to the first day of the week? Even in our Armenian language the sixth day was called a preparation day. Preparation for what? they wondered.

Our landlord, Halis *Effendy*, happened to overhear the conversation. He expressed an interest; so I lost no time in seizing the opportunity of witnessing to this Muslim gentleman. I reached for my Turkish Bible and opened to Exodus 20. I read the Ten Commandments and then led into a discussion of this supreme moral code. I offered to get a Turkish Bible for Halis *Effendy* if he would promise to read it. This he readily agreed to do.

Sometime later a woman we had known in Sultaniye met Mother on the street. "I hear that your son-in-law is coming here," the woman said.

"What son-in-law?" Mother queried. "I have one in the army in Jerusalem. He surely can't be coming. The other one died in the Death March."

"Oh, that nice young man with the Russians in Sultaniye—the one we called Lucky Boy."

"He is not my son-in-law," Mother declared. "Mary is not married!"

The other woman nodded and smiled knowingly as she went on her way.

That same day Papa Paul brought the mail from the post office. He brought a bundle of letters that had been forwarded to us from Sultaniye. One from my brother-in-law, Onnig Pirenian in Jerusalem, expressed his hope of an end to the sad conditions we all endured. Among the others was a letter from Yagof Egitkhanoff. He had been taking care of our mail ever since we left the town. His letter did not mention anything about the possibility that he would be coming to Konya. It was merely a polite note about the mail he had sent.

But this eventful day held still another surprise. A friend came to tell me that someone at the American hospital had some letters for me. She said that I would have to go for the letters personally; so I went with her.

As we entered the hospital grounds, I saw a man, who looked somewhat familiar, sitting on a bench. The man stood up and turned to meet us. Baron Lucky! Yagof Egitkhanoff! But, oh, how he had changed in the months since we had last seen each other. The dread malaria had worn him down and left him weak and emaciated.

Yagof had two letters for me: one contained a little money. He also gave me a small package of fresh country butter. How kind of him to remember Mother and me in such a practical way.

One day in the last week of March, *Digin* Nunufar Shakerjian asked me to help her mend some lace curtains for the Kurdish officer, Ali Riza. Hysmig, Digin Nunufar Shakerjian's teenage daughter, worked with us. Our fingers flew, and soon the job was finished. Just then Ali Riza's daughter, Henduhie, came in and asked Hysmig and me to go for a walk with her. Neither of us really wanted to go, but Henduhie insisted; so we decided to humor her. I would have to go home and change clothes first, because I was not dressed for walking in public, I told the two girls.

As I neared the gate to our yard, I saw a little girl enter. Close behind her was Yagof! Seeing this unexpected visitor suddenly changed my plans for a walk. I turned and ran back toward the Shakerjians's residence to tell the other girls that I could not go with them.

Apparently Yagof had seen me and thought I was trying to run away from him; so he started after me. When *Digin* Nunufar opened the door in answer to my knock, she saw Yagof behind me. She stepped out and invited him to enter; she wanted to talk with him for a minute she said.

Digin Nunufar began to praise my good qualities, and Baron Lucky could not conceal his admiration. I felt most embarrassed and uneasy.

Just then Mehmed (the pseudo Kurd) came in. Upon seeing the stranger, he did not know quite how to react. But *Digin* Nunufar introduced the two young men—a Kurd and a Russian citizen. Quickly, however, the correct nationality surfaced, and the two began to share their experiences and their similar circumstances.

But Yagof wanted to visit me in my temporary

home. In order to make everything proper and avoid arousing any suspicions, I went home alone. Moments later *Digin* Nunufar accompanied Yagof. Once inside the main gate, I waited, and the three of us entered the house together. We introduced Yagof to the Boghosians (Mother was not there at the time), and he began to explain his presence in Konya.

The unwholesome conditions in Sultaniye had so affected Yagof that he was actually in danger of death. The humane governor, the gentle official who had snatched our family of seven from the Death March, had sent Yagof to Konya in the governor's own carriage. The terrible situation in that town had deteriorated since we had left. Disease and starvation stalked the streets and invaded the miserable hovels where our people tried to maintain the slender thread of life.

The next day Yagof returned for another short visit and found me wrapped in my large shawl. Any little excitement or worry brought on the chills and fever of the malaria that my body harbored.

Yagof quizzed me on our living conditions. I could not tell him that because of him our small aid from the Near East Relief had been cut off. Someone had written to the office in Istanbul that I was engaged to a rich young man who was sending me 200 *kouroush* a month. What a lot of harm some idle gossip was causing. Now Mother and I had a hard time scraping together enough money to buy a little food. Mother worked in the vineyards when she was able, and I worked once in a while at the German headquarters. But I could not tell Yagof all this. I would not give him any excuse to make us obliged to him for aid. I told him only that we managed to get along.

The two of us were seated on the bench in the garden behind our landlord's home—the first time we had been alone. We both talked for a few minutes about the beauties of nature—the trees and flowers and the half moon that hung in the sky overhead.

Suddenly Yagof said quietly, "Mary, could you think of me and try to like me?" He paused a moment. "I need you!" he declared almost pathetically.

"Yes," I said, "I worry about you." I paused a moment and then added, "You do need help, but I think the help you need is somewhat different from what you have in mind." I looked into his eyes and said as earnestly as I could, "Yagof, you need to know Jesus and turn your life over to Him."

Yagof stood up and faced me. "I was freed miraculously three times from certain death. God sent me to Sultaniye so that I could deliver you from the traps that were set for you." He spread his arms as if he were an orator reaching the climax of an impassioned speech. "Mary," he implored, "can't you see? Before God our Father I believe that you belong to me." He paused. "Mary, please—! Won't you promise to be my life companion?"

I sat speechless, trembling all over. I felt as if my body were being buffeted in a rough sea about to engulf me. How could I help this young man find peace when both of us faced hazards every moment? How could I turn his mind to the only real source of comfort—our loving Saviour? How could I consent to marry someone who did not share my precious Seventh-day Adventist faith? The struggle raged in my mind without any apparent solution.

"Mary," Yagof said softly, "say something."

"Yagof, it is certainly true that God has spared our lives and brought us together here, but we do not know what the future holds," I began. "Why should we ask anyone else to face our tribulations?" I groped for words. "If your heart has an empty place for God's love to cure your hurt—"

He would not let me finish. He took my cold hands in his own and bowed his head over our clasped hands. "Mary," he whispered, "you must trust. You must scatter your doubts and believe." He lifted his head and looked into my eyes. Then he said "There is no fear in love," as he slowly released my hands.

I stood up and shivered in the cool evening air.

Yagof politely took his leave and was gone.

I stood in the moonlit garden and tried to believe that it had not all been a kind of pleasant dream tinged with sadness. I wondered when and how I would see him again.

Unlucky Baron Lucky

Yagof came again on the following Sunday afternoon. I had attended services at the Protestant church that morning and stopped for a short visit with friends on the way home. When I entered the house, I found visitors waiting for me—Yagof and another young man, Gabris Yeramian, also a Russian citizen.

I greeted them in the traditional Armenian fashion for the Easter season by shaking hands and saying, "Christ is risen from the dead."

The two young men wanted to see the garden in the landlord's yard. Gabris said that Yagof had described the lovely spot. Of course we had permission to enter the garden whenever we wished, but I felt that I should obtain permission to take strangers there if the family were at home. Also, if the Turkish owners were present, we should not have men and women there at the same time.

The Turkish family were away from home, so the three of us entered the garden. For a few minutes we walked around, admiring the beauty. Then Gabris suddenly decided to go back into the house to visit with Mother and the others. Obviously, the two men had planned the whole procedure.

Yagof and I sat on the bench where, only a few

evenings before, he had proposed marriage.

Now he had a lot to say, and the words tumbled out in a torrent. *Digin* Nunufar, apparently had urged him not to give up on me. He wanted me to have a picture taken and give him a print. He spoke of his plans to make life more comfortable for me—and him. "Mary," he said solemnly, "I vow before God our Father that I will remain true to you whatever happens. Will you promise the same—to save me from death?"

Again I hesitated. "Yagof, things are too uncertain now. We do not know what tomorrow may bring. Can you be sure that even this very day you will be allowed to remain here in Konya?"

"True enough, Mary." He bowed his head sadly. "I will probably be sent back to Sultaniye. But that does not change the vow I made a moment ago. God willing, when this madness ends, I will find you and we will be happy together."

"We must leave the future in God's hands," I agreed.

"You will write to me, won't you Mary?"

"Yes, I will write." I stood up. "Yagof, we must return to the house now. We must not give anyone occasion to talk about our conduct." And we went back to join the others.

Mother and the Boghosians had prepared a simple meal of such food as we had. Fortunately, we had some eggs to supplement a potato stew and a few other things. But Yagof seemed to have no appetite at all. He appeared quite agitated.

Monday morning *Digin* Nunufar called me to help her again, this time to make some dresses for Ali Riza's wife. When I returned home for lunch, shocking news greeted me.

Yagof had been jailed!

A younger brother of Gabris had come to tell us of the arrest. It seems that Turkish authorities had made a sweep to round up recent escapees from Sultaniye, and they considered Yagof one of them. Now all of them were in jail awaiting deportation.

What could I do? All sorts of ideas popped into my head. Should I go to the jail and try to cheer the unfortunate prisoners? If I did that, the officers might question me and discover my status. Then I would be clapped into the jail with the others.

In my frenzy and uncertainty I ran back to *Digin* Nunufar's house and told her what had happened. Perhaps Ali Riza or one of his subordinate officers could intercede with the Turkish police and secure Yagof's release.

As I entered the gate to the Shakerjian place, Mehmed came out of the mansion to speak to me. He wanted me to speak to Hysmig in his behalf. "Mehmed," I exclaimed, "this is no time to talk of romance. Yagof is in jail!"

"Yagof!" Mehmed gasped. "In jail? Why?"

"They're going to send him back to Sultaniye." I explained. "I thought maybe Ali Riza or one of the other officers might help. At least they might get him out of jail and let him go back to Sultaniye on his own rather than as a prisoner."

"I'll take care of that myself right now," Mehmed declared. "Then you can talk to Hysmig."

"I'll see about Hysmig later," I promised. "The immediate concern is to get Yagof out of jail."

I forgot all about being hungry. I waited at *Digin* Nunufar's house for two hours for information. Then Mehmed returned, so exhausted and upset that he could hardly talk. He himself had been beaten and cast into jail!

Mehmed had gone to the chief of police for permission to visit Yagof. "You are a Kurd, and he is a Russian." the chief said. "How do you know him?" The officer looked at Mehmed narrowly. "Where and when did you two meet?"

"Sir, we had been acquainted in Van, and here we met on the street," Mehmed lied. "I would ask your kindness to release him from jail and allow him to stay with me until he can arrange to return to Sultaniye. He did come here with permission, you know."

"You come and sit in my chair if you are so smart," the officer snorted. "We don't know for sure that this Russian has any permit from the governor to be here. Maybe you are a runaway too." And he ordered the jailer to lock Mehmed up with the others. Because the young man resisted, the jailer beat him into submission.

Fortunately another Turkish policeman came in shortly. This man knew Mehmed, and this officer intervened to have Mehmed released.

What a disappointment! Mehmed had not even been allowed to speak with Yagof.

For quite a while we discussed what had happened and tried to formulate some kind of plan for freeing Yagof. But we seemed to talk in circles and come back to the frustrating reality that nothing could be done. Toward evening Mehmed was summoned by telephone to appear at the police headquarters and sign various papers to clear himself. Finally I returned to my house to spend an almost sleepless night.

Early on Tuesday morning several of us went to Gabris Yeramian's house to see if any further news had come. Gabris and his parents had tried all day Monday to get Yagof released, but to no avail. They did learn, however, the reasons for the arrest. It seems that Yagof had registered at a hotel on his arrival in Konya. Then he had met his friends, the Yeramians, who invited him to stay with them. So the authorities, checking records, concluded that, because he had not stayed in the hotel, he was trying to disappear.

During the few days Yagof had spent in Konya, he had spoken to the principal of the Turkish technical school. He had applied for a job teaching the boys the art of sewing the upper parts for shoes. When the principal heard of Yagof's arrest, he went to the authorities. "I need that boy," he declared. "He has a skill I want in my school." But even this appeal proved fruitless.

Toward evening of that black day, Yagof was taken from the jail—not free, but in chains as a common criminal between two burly guards. They boarded a train for Eregli, from whence they would proceed by carriage to Sultaniye. Yagof had to pay 80 *kouroush* for railroad tickets, provide food for three and hire the carriage for himself and his two guards.

A few days later I received a card from Yagof. He had arrived safely in Sultaniye, and he was trying to secure permission to leave again.

That same day news reached Konya that the United States had entered the war on the side of the Allies. There would be no more money from the Near East Relief.

All Armenian boys aged 12 to 17 must now enter an army youth program to receive military training twice a week.

Armenian women were advised to dress decently in public. Sadly to say, some had sold their honor in order to save their lives. Women were to avoid walking abroad alone or at night. They should not join in any parties for pleasure.

Bread now became in short supply, especially in the big cities. Rationing was to be much more strictly enforced.

We did not know for sure what was happening in the world outside Turkey. Rumors of violent naval warfare in the Mediterranean filtered through. Some said that the British had cleared the lower Tigris River and in March captured Baghdad more than 300 miles inland. Other British action threatened Palestine; most Turkish civilians had been evacuated from Jerusalem, although the military, including my brother-in-law Onnig Pirenian, still remained there. The Russian drive south through the Caucasus had halted. Nobody seemed to know why, but rumors insisted that the United States had offered Russia huge sums of money if the invasion would continue. Perhaps, the rumors speculated, the Russians might overrun all of Anatolia, including Konya.

Certainly we lived in uncertain times. But, praise God, we were still alive, and our trust in the Lord was unshaken.

Baron Lucky Again

The beautiful weather of late March and early April dissolved into day after day of cold rain. The damp floor of our guesthouse turned to mud, and the walls almost dripped water. We had no way to warm the single living room, the only fireplace being in the small "kitchen" hole in the wall across the entrance hall. Only by going to bed could we keep warm. Such conditions, coupled with insufficient food, caused the ever-present malaria to flare up again. One or more of us in that exile home seemed to be down most of the time.

Eventually the cold, rainy days gave way to warmer weather, and our health improved again. As the days passed, letters arrived quite regularly from Sultaniye. Requests for medicine, which I purchased with the money that accompanied the letters, alternated with pathetic accounts of conditions in that place I always thought of as the "graveyard of the living dead" and hopeful declarations of intent to get back to Konya.

About the middle of May I received word that a bundle had been sent from Yagof by a trusted messenger to the inn where most of such traffic was handled. When I went to claim the bundle, the man in charge professed to be unaware of anything there for me. I knew the man was lying; he wanted to keep whatever it was because of its value. Finally Papa Paul went with me, and after a confrontation, the man brought out the bundle, a sack of expensive Angora goats' wool. This wool, after it was washed and dried, Mother would spin into fine yarn for making valuable articles to sell.

On the evening of that day I had gone to a friend's house nearby to read some letters for them and write replies. I noticed that it had started to rain, and I had decided to run home before the rain came down harder. But one of the young men present said he had recently been in Sultaniye and had seen Yagof. Yagof was trying hard to get a permit to return to Konya. "I would run away from that hell if I could, regardless of the consequences," he was quoted as declaring.

At that moment Mother hurried in to call for me. "Someone is waiting for you, dear," she panted. "Hurry and go home."

What a surprise greeted me as I dashed in the door. There sat Yagof, talking with the Boghosians. I couldn't believe my eyes. I stood in the door for a moment, speechless.

"What—? How—?" I gasped. "Yagof! Where did you come from?"

"Well, Mary," he answered, a twinkle in his eyes, "I just dropped in to let you know I'm still able to get around."

"Don't joke with me!" I said. "Why are you here?"

"Well, to tell the truth, I'm here by orders of the government of Turkey." He smiled broadly, savoring my reaction.

"The government?" I gulped.

"Yes," he affirmed. "I was just telling Papa Paul that the government has ordered eight of us Russians sent to a better climate for our health. We are here in Konya awaiting transfer to another detention center at

Beysehir." Beysehir I knew was about fifty miles southwest of Konya at the south end of Lake Beysehir.

"Then you will be leaving again soon?" Despite my determination not to show emotion, my voice quavered.

"I didn't say that, my dear." He spoke seriously now. "The group is under orders to leave in a day or so, but I intend to stay here if at all possible. I am going to try again to get a teaching position at the Turkish technical school."

"Oh, I hope—" I choked back a sob. "Let's pray that God's will may be done."

The next day, Sabbath, Yagof came again quite early in the afternoon. Since the Turkish family were away for the summer, we had free use of their yard, and Yagof and I sat on the bench for a long time in the warm sunshine of early summer.

"I am told you have a recent photograph of yourself," Yagof said abruptly.

"Well, yes," I admitted. "I did have one taken a few weeks ago."

"Please, let me see it," he pleaded.

I went into the house and brought out the picture, a wallet-size portrait.

"Oh," Yagof sighed. "You remind me so much of my dear departed sister." He reached out suddenly and snatched the picture from my hand. He regarded it tenderly for a moment; then, with a quick motion, he tucked it into his wallet.

"Yagof!" I exploded. "Give me back my picture!"

"All right," he said agreeably. He took out his wallet, pulled out a dog-eared picture, and handed it to me—the class picture of my junior year in school that had been given him in Sultaniye.

What could I do? A lump rose up in my throat and tears came to my eyes. "Yagof—" I began.

"Marichen," he said, using the endearing form of my name, "you wouldn't deprive me of this small remembrance, would you?" He looked so forlorn that I could not bring myself to be harsh.

"No, Yagof," I sighed, "you may keep it."

Words cannot convey the turmoil that wracked my mind in the days that followed. For some reason Yagof and the group of Russians did not receive orders to leave Konya. Day after day Yagof worked on permission to stay, and evening after evening he visited us, or we went together to visit some of the nearby families in our part of town. He sweetly but persistently pressured me to make an affirmative answer to his proposal. I could not bring myself to make a commitment. How could I give up my determination to gain more education and be of value in the Lord's work? How could the two of us face the complicated uncertainties of life in exile? How could he, officially a Russian citizen, albeit an Armenian, marry an Armenian girl in direct violation of Turkish law? The obstacles loomed before me with such formidability that I felt chilled through and through as I thought about it.

One afternoon I met Yagof unexpectedly in the home of the Azarian sisters.

"Mary," he said, "Pastor Agasian sent word that he wants to see me at his home. Would you mind going with me?"

"Oh," I answered, "it isn't far from here. I can tell you how to find the place."

"I'm sure you could." He spoke in his quiet, disarming way. "I'd much rather have you show me the way than tell me." He hesitated to see if I would answer. "Doesn't your sister's brother-in-law, Gabriel Pirenian, live in the same yard?"

"True," I answered.

"You could visit his family too," he continued.

So Yagof and I walked together through the narrow streets of the Turkish quarter the two long blocks to the house where the Pirenians and the Agasians lived.

Just as we reached the gate, a peddler came along the street selling fresh mulberries. Yagof stopped and bought two bags of the delicious fruit, one for Gabriel's family and one for the pastor's family. How we enjoyed the treat as we sat together in the Agasian's room.

Abruptly Pastor Agasian declared, "I wrote a letter to Gabriel's brother Onnig in Jerusalem. We informed him that Mary is being engaged to marry a good young man, a proper person."

Yagof's face beamed.

I cannot describe my feelings of confusion. Was I being framed? I had not given anyone an indication that I had accepted Yagof's proposal. Was this God's way of telling me to accept? Or was the devil trying to trap me in a snare from which I could not escape?

Then Yagof told us some good news that he had withheld until this opportune time. "I have been accepted to teach at the technical school, and I have official permission to stay in Konya!"

I had never seen the young man so elated. He exuded a confidence that everything was working out precisely right.

"I am going to rent a room near the school," he continued. Turning to me he said, "I want you and your mother to move there first, and then I will join you later."

I looked down at the toes of my shoes. In a voice that hardly seemed my own I said, "I must first ask my mother's consent."

Pastor Agasian broke into the conversation. "Perhaps it may be possible to arrange with the Russian government for the support of the two women. On the other hand," he added,"nobody seems to know what kind of conditions exist in Russia. In any case, we should probably arrange for a wedding before too long in order to avoid difficulties."

Pastor Agasian paused and nodded gravely at my look of consternation. "You see, Mary," he continued, "your name appears on Yagof's residence permit as his wife."

Lightning could not have shocked me more if it had made a direct hit on that house.

"What?" I gasped.

Pastor Agasian took a paper from Yagof's hand and held it out for me to see. It had the official stamp of the local Turkish authorities. No doubt at all, it was Yagof's registration paper. The pastor pointed to a line that read "Baron Hagop (Russian form of Jacob) Egitkhanoff and his *zevjesie* Mary." Then he asked, "What does *zevjesie* mean, Mary?" He knew that I could read Turkish very well.

"Wife," I gulped. "How—"

"Just a moment, Mary," the pastor cut in. "Let Yagof explain."

"Well, I vow that this was not my doing, Mary." Yagof wore a solemn and utterly sincere expression. "The old clerk, partially deaf and obviously not too well educated asked me, 'Young man, do you have anyone else with you?' I answered, 'Well, my fiancée, Mary, lives in Konya.' Then I saw him write what you see here. I did not know what he had written until he handed me the completed paper. Now I realize that he didn't know the meaning of the word fiancée.

We sat in stunned silence looking at that document with the word that should not be there.

Thoughts tumbled through my brain. Could this be an act of providential guidance? One of my chief concerns from the very first acquaintance with Yagof had been the fact that he did not share with me the same precious faith. How could I consent to be "unequally yoked together" with an unbeliever. Of course he protested that he was a believer, and in a sense he was. He had been brought up in a Christian home. But he did not understand the distinctive truths of God's Word concerning the blessed hope of Christ's soon return and the necessity to observe the seventh-day Sabbath. He did have a mild and lovable nature, and he did like to study the Bible.

Another serious concern had been the Turkish law forbidding the marriage of Armenian girls to foreigners. Now my name appeared on a government document as this man's wife. What would happen to him—to me—if he should try having this clerical error corrected? We might both be sent back to Sultaniye into exile where I would be fair game for that tiger of a postmaster. I felt that I had fallen into a quagmire from which I could in no way crawl out. What would happen now?

Pastor Agasian called for Gabriel to come down from his upstairs apartment, and the three men continued to discuss the best way to handle the situation. I soon stood up to leave. I was so upset that I could not endure any more talk. I bade them all good-bye, and Gabriel's daughter walked home with me.

In my distress I sought the Lord in prayer.

Meanwhile preparations went ahead for a party to announce our engagement. Yagof introduced me to the Khachadouroffs and the Magosoffs, two Russian-Armenian families living near him. The Khachadouroffs immediately determined to be a godfather and godmother to us at our engagement and at the wedding.

It was absolutely essential that Yagof find a better place to live. The tiny room he lived in would not be at all adequate for Mother and me to move in with him.

The Khachadouroffs wanted him to find a place near them, but none was available. He felt he should be near the school. Finding a place to live loomed up as a serious obstacle.

One day Sirarpy Boghosian, a niece of Papa Paul, came in. She suggested that I go with her to see if we could find a place to rent. We went directly to the neighborhood of the school. Oddly enough, we two girls succeeded where everyone else had failed. We found a vacant guesthouse better than any we had seen anywhere. The owner was willing to rent it at a reasonable price. This house, like all others, consisted of a single room adjoining the camel barn; but that room was spacious! It had a wooden floor seven steps up from the dirt passageway. The outside wall had three windows and a door that opened onto a glassed-in sun porch. And the room was dry. This guesthouse had its own walled yard separate from the main yard.

Sirarpy and I hurried back to report our discovery, and who should be at the house but Yagof! Of course he wanted to see the place immediately.

Without further delay Yagof arranged for the rent. He hired a carriage from the landlord to move mother's and my belongings. It was already late afternoon, so Mother and I quickly bundled up our few things, loaded them into the carriage, and rode in style to our new home. For the first time in the two years since we locked our door in Bardezag, we lived in uncramped quarters and in relative comfort. It did not take us long to store our few meager possessions in the large closets, and we retired early so that we could have a good rest. The next day, we knew, promised excitement that would tax our energies to the limit.

Countdown to "I Do"

Mother and I awoke with the dawn. We had so much to do that we could hardly wait for daylight. The house must be made spotlessly clean. We had no fancy furniture or drapes, so we had to depend on flawless cleanliness to make our home presentable. The three large windows, though not really dirty, must sparkle. I tackled that job first.

Yagof would come soon after noon, and guests would arrive at two o'clock. The Khachadouroffs and the Magosoffs, as well as another Russian family, the Batoumtziks were invited. Pastor and Mrs. Agasian and Gabriel's family would come. Mother had sent word to my niece Naomi, Sirarpy Boghosian, and some others. My sister Heripsime was ill in the hospital at the time.

Later in the day Mrs. Khachadouroff led me to the front of the room, and the buzz of conversation died down. She called Yagof to join us. She had us join hands while she wished us many blessings and announced that congratulations were now in order for our engagement. The moment had arrived—Friday afternoon, July 20, 1917.

Our friends pressed around to shower their blessing on us—the men jovial and hearty with their congratulations, and most of the women with glistening eyes and tremulous voices. It was an emotional occasion that left our hearts warm with the genuine friendship everyone exhibited.

Yagof asked us to have our Adventist families meet in our home the next day. He said he wanted to meet with us. This, of course made me very happy, and fellowship with the believers provided strengthening support.

On Monday one of my young friends came to the house and offered to help me sew a shirt for Yagof and a wedding dress for me. She was known as an expert seamstress, so I gladly accepted her offer. We went together to buy material, but we returned with only two yards—enough for one shirt—for which we paid 40 *kouroush* a yard. At that price, enough material for a wedding dress would cost almost a thousand *kouroush*. How could I spend that much for a dress, even if I did have the money? With thousands of my people living in peril of their lives, malnourished or starving, trying to cover their nakedness with pitiful rags, I simply could not think of spending money for an extravagant dress. The shirt would be useful after the wedding, but a wedding dress— I didn't know what I would do, but I made up my mind that I would not spend money foolishly.

We had borrowed a portable sewing machine from our new landlady, so we went to work on the shirt. I laid out the material and the pattern and cut out the pieces. My friend sewed the seams. But there was a problem. Her fiancé had found out where she was and he had invited himself in.

With him sitting beside her, she had her mind on something other than making straight seams. She sewed; I ripped. Nothing was done right. By noon we had only a half-finished shirt, and that not correct.

Yagof dropped by for lunch. He was not pleased. "Marichen," he said quietly but positively taking me aside, "take it all apart and start over. Do the work by yourself. I am sure that you can do better alone."

My "helper" did not return after that. She had to find some other place for a rendezvous with her young man.

One Sunday in July, Yagof went with me and several other girls to visit *Digin* Nunufar Shekerjian. Her daughter Heranoush was there with her husband Gregore Katarjian. These people expressed genuine interest in finding out how Yagof had managed to survive the hazards and make his way to Konya. They pressed him for his story. When he said that it hurt him to relive those painful experiences, they urged him to keep on, insisting that it would be good for him to purge his mind by bringing out into the open all the haunting memories that plagued him.

Under this gentle and understanding concern, Yagof told his story.

His parents, who were godly Christians, made their home in Erzurum, near the Russian border. Many Armenians lived in Russian territory and had Russian names. Yagof's grandfather had received the name Egitkhanoff as an honor award from the tsar for bravery. (*Egit* means "brave"; *khan* means "home"—"home of the brave.") Yagof himself had lived for eight years with his grandmother in Kars, then in Russian territory. It was there that he had learned the trade of shoemaking as well as fluency in the Russian language.

In 1914 Yagof returned to Erzurum and opened his own business of making shoes. He became engaged to the daughter of a wealthy family, and life promised to be easy and pleasant. Then the war broke out. Air castles tumbled. A mad scramble for mere survival soon crowded out all other considerations.

Yagof urged his aged mother to flee to Russia, as many others were doing, while it was possible to do so; but she refused to leave her married daughters and their families. Turkish repression soon closed in. Yagof and his mother had their Russian citizenship papers taken away, and they then became Turkish Armenians. When evacuation of Armenians from frontier areas began, they joined, but at different times, the more than thirty thousand people of Erzurum forced out of their homes. Yagof never saw his mother, two of his sisters, or his fiancée again.

Then followed a recital of the atrocities with which we were all too familiar: brutal beatings, massacres, forced marches, starvation, and all the rest. Yagof, with probably six thousand others, left Erzurum. Six months later about forty or fifty of that vast number arrived in Aleppo. Three times Yagof had been tied up with men destined for slaughter; three times he had been delivered miraculously. He saw men pushed off cliffs while their women below watched the bodies pile up in twisted masses, some still alive and moaning pitiously. He saw guards hack off fingers from marchers in order to take their gold rings or knock out teeth to get the gold caps or fillings. When he crossed a ford in the Euphrates River, he had to push floating bodies out of the way. He would never be able to erase from his mind the horrors of that dreadful march.

When he reached Aleppo, his fluency in Russian and Turkish proved to be his salvation. A group of Russian prisoners of war needed an interpreter to deal with Turkish officials. Yagof was given forged documents of Russian citizenship and attached to the Russian prisoners. That was how he arrived in Sultaniye. That was the providential circumstance behind our meeting.

The emotional drain of reliving these terrible experiences left Yagof exhausted. *Digin* Nunufar brought in some fresh apricots and some other refreshments. After an interval of relaxation and pleasant conversation, Yagof and I rose to leave. Our friends now kept urging us to avoid a long delay in consumating our marriage.

I still had no wedding dress, but one day a package came from my sister Varsenig in Eskisehir. Upon opening the package, I couldn't believe my eyes. There, with a few other things, lay my white graduation dress. No letter of explanation came with the package, but I learned later that a friendly neighbor in Bardezag had seen the dress in our house when the Turkish officials had been looting our place. On an impulse she had grabbed it and then managed to deliver it to Varsenig. The dress was not elaborate, but it would do very nicely for the wedding. In fact, the dressmaker had predicted just such a possibility. "Mary," she had said, "I have an idea. I'm going to leave enough material turned up for the hem so that later you can let it out and have a long dress." She chuckled pleasantly. "Who knows?" she said with a twinkle in her eye. "You may even want to wear this for your wedding."

Well, that simple white dress was not exactly what I had in mind for my wedding; but with the high cost of material and the shortage of money, I could see that here was the answer to my prayers. With a veil and crown for my head and a bouquet of fresh flowers to carry in my hands, the dress would serve very well. Yagof would be wearing nothing new either, except for the shirt I had made.

But the providential arrival of a dress did not solve our problem. For Yagof still had no income. For four months he had not received an allowance from Russia; and for four months he had worked without pay in the Turkish school. His small reserve of cash was about exhausted. Something had to be done.

Finally Yagof decided to speak to the principal of the school about the possibility of receiving a small salary for his work. "I have worked here four months," he said. "I have worn my own clothes and shoes. I have provided my own food. Now my clothes and shoes are wearing out, and my food is finished. Also I have two other mouths to feed. I'm sure you understand, *effendy*."

"Yagof, *effendy,* you were headed for a prison camp with the other Russian prisoners when you came here. Is not that correct?"

"Yes, *effendy*."

"I did you a favor and arranged for you to stay here instead of going into exile. Isn't that enough?" The principal frowned, but he did not wait for a reply. "You said you would work here without pay—which you have done. Now you have a choice: either continue the present arrangement or join your countrymen wherever they are."

"Thank you, *effendy*," Yagof said quietly. "I will have to make a petition to the governor."

Two days later Mother went with another woman to the jail. They often went there to give something to the boys who were being sent off into exile. Imagine her surprise to find Yagof there.

"Oh, Mother Ebross!" he exclaimed. "God must have sent you here today. Please have Mary tell the Khachadouroffs that I am here. Maybe they can get me out."

"Yagof!" Mother gasped. "Why are you here?"

"It's because of my petition," Yagof explained. "As soon as it reached headquarters, an order was issued to arrest me and send me to Beysehir where the other Russian prisoners are."

Mother hurried home to tell me of this disturbing turn of events, and I went immediately to the Khachadouroffs' place.

Mr. Khachadouroff was not at home, but their nineteen-year-old son, Garo, was there. He went with me to the courthouse to see what could be done. We were shunted from one officer to another without any success. Finally we went to the jail and obtained permission to talk with Yagof, surrounded by policemen.

Poor Yagof! He stood there pale, shivering, frightened, and worried. Obviously his malaria had flared up. Although it was only September, the weather had turned chilly, and the jail was cold.

Garo and I went out and bought a little food for Yagof. Then we hurried home to get his coat. When we returned, the guards would not allow us to enter. They took the coat. We hurried away again to get a blanket and a pillow. I also brought my big shawl.

As we approached the jail, we were surprised to hear Yagof's voice calling out to us. We looked up and saw him at a window. The bottom half of the windows had been boarded up, but anyone on the inside could see through cracks between the boards. Yagof had been watching, and when he saw us coming he managed to climb up on something and call out from the top part of the windows. He told us that he could not even lie down because of lice all over the benches in his cell. "Please get someone to sponsor me so that I can spend the night somewhere else," he pleaded.

We returned to the Khachadouroff's place, and Barour, Garo's younger brother, ran off to find their father. When the older Khachadouroff came in out of breath, and at the same time Mother came limping in to see what had happened to me, we all decided to go to the jailer and request that Yagof be released for the night.

Come back in the morning," the officer grunted. "He must stay here tonight." He dismissed us with a wave of his hand.

As a guard opened the outside door for us, he said quietly, "Why don't you get a good night's rest and come early in the morning? The officer in charge of bails will be here then. You will find him more gracious."

We talked to Yagof again through the window. We tried to encourage him by the hope that something could be done in the morning. We bade him good-night and committed him to the care of our heavenly Father. Then we all left—the Khachadouroffs to their place, and Mother and I to ours. Mother fixed some food, but neither of us could eat. We went to bed but could not sleep.

Again confusing thoughts chased each other around and around in my tortured brain.

My name on Yagof's permit as his wife—and we were not even married.

Maybe officers would drag me out of bed to go with him.

Mother left by herself. What would she do?

Suppose I told them I was not his wife. Then would they send him off to prison camp and me back to Sultaniye—or worse?

What if—? And so it went all night except for fitful snatches of sleep.

The next morning early I took a lunch for Yagof—bread, cheese, raisins—and went to the jail.

"Good morning, Sweetie," he called through the cracks in the boarded up window. "Do you have any news yet?"

"No, Yagof," I said. "Nothing. Mr. Khachadouroff has talked with other Russian people. They do not know of anything to do." I heard Yagof sigh—almost a sob. "Don't be discouraged," I added quickly. Maybe something will happen yet. Perhaps I should talk to the principal of the school."

"Oh, no, Marichen, don't do that!" Yagof paused. "Oh, look, Mary, look! There goes Mr. Dapchevich. He is the only one who might know what to do."

I looked toward the street, but I could not tell which man was Mr. Dapchevich.

"He is just entering the cafe," Yagof said. "Run, Mary! Hurry!"

How could I tell Yagof that Mr. Khachadouroff had already talked to Mr. Dapchevich? How could I now face this man when he had said the case was hopeless?

"Oh, Mary," Yagof urged, "go quickly! He can help."

Now, Mr. Dapchevich did not speak or understand Turkish very well and Armenian not at all. I could not handle Russian. He did, however, speak French; but my French was extremely limited.

Did it just happen that a friend of the Azarian sisters came along the street just then—and she spoke French very well?

I approached the woman and asked her to go with me, and she agreed. We entered the cafe and found Mr. Dapchevich seated at one of the tables. We spoke to him and began to explain the situation.

"Oh, ladies," he said politely, "please allow me to get chairs for you." He quickly brought two chairs. "Now please be seated. We can discuss the business much better that way."

We briefly told the gentleman the background of the case, and I appealed for whatever assistance he could give.

"Ladies," he said, "I'm not sure that I can do anything for this unfortunate young man."

A deep sigh escaped my lips.

"I'll tell you what," Mr. Dapchevich said. "I'll go with you to the jail. Maybe I can talk to someone there."

The three of us went to the jail. Yagof must have been waiting and watching for me to return, for we suddenly heard him calling "Oh, honorable sir, please go inside at once. The ladies had better wait outside."

After we had waited for what seemed like an interminable time, Mr. Dapchevich came out—actually, we learned, only about fifteen minutes later.

"I spoke to the chief," the gentleman told us. "He advised Baron Egitkhanoff to submit another petition." He bowed to us politely. "Please let me know this afternoon how things turn out."

I went to a Turkish lawyer whom I knew to be friendly and asked him to draw up a proper petition. I signed Yagof's Russian name, Baron Hagop Egitkhanoff. For this service I paid 15 *kouroush*—money we needed for food. I took the paper and showed it to Yagof through the window.

"That's fine," he assured me. "Now have Garo take it to the office of the lieutenant governor."

I took the petition to the Khachadouroff home and asked Garo to deliver it for me. Then I went home to prepare some nourishing food for Yagof.

My good friend Nevart Azarian came by. She was shocked to hear of Yagof's arrest, and she offered to help in any way she could. I asked her to go with me so that I would not have to be on the streets alone.

We took the food to the jail. Then we went to the Khachadouroffs to find out if Garo had been successful, but he had not returned. We were walking along the street, trying to decide what to do next, when Garo came running toward us.

"There is no hope," he panted. "It seems that Yagof must be sent to the detention camp where the other Russian prisoners are." He handed me the petition. "I couldn't get anyone to take it. Everyone is afraid of his own head.

I looked at the petition, and tears welled up in my eyes. How utterly helpless I felt.

"Never mind, Mary." Nevart put her arm around me and drew my head to her shoulder. "Don't give up. Let's take that petition to the courthouse and find the right person to take it."

Dear, loyal friend! She was willing to go with me into the "lion's den"!

We went back to the jail and talked to Yagof through the window. He encouraged us to go directly to the lieutenant governor's office.

Up the stairs we went. A secretary stopped us and asked us our business. He took the petition, signed it, and motioned for us to go into an office. There we found several men seated at different desks. We had no idea which one should see the petition. Someone took the paper from me and glanced at it. He handed it to someone else, who handed it on. Finally one of the men opened a book and made some kind of notation. Then they all began to question me, and I tried to explain why Yagof was in jail.

One of the officers suddenly spoke up. "The young man had a right to complain. Nobody should be expected to work for our government without pay."

Then all the men began to discuss the matter among themselves. One of the men, I learned, was the clerk who had put my name on Yagof's paper as "wife"! They all expressed their sympathy.

The man who had started the discussion said to me, "Go down to the jail and tell Yagof that if he will agree to go back to work free, he will be released. In about two weeks something should be worked out about pay."

We went back downstairs to the jail, and the jailer allowed us to talk with Yagof. We told him about our conversation with the secretaries. It seems that the supervisor of the shoemaking department had advised Yagof to return to the job without pressing the matter further. That man and the lawyer who drew up the petition were at that moment negotiating with the chief of police for Yagof's release.

"Take the petition to the chief's office," Yagof told us.

Back upstairs, we went to the police department. A clerk took the petition from me, saw that it was properly signed, and handed it back.

"Are you the man's wife?" he said in a mocking tone of voice, an evil grin on his face. Without waiting for my answer, he motioned toward a door. "Take this paper in there," he said. The other men in the room nodded knowingly, winking and smiling at each other.

With a prayer on our lips and fear in our hearts we started toward the door. Just as we were about to enter, the door opened and out stepped the shoemaking supervisor and the lawyer.

"Here, young ladies," said the supervisor, "let me have that petition. I'll take care of the business from here on. You go back downstairs and wait a few minutes. We'll have this all settled before long."

In the waiting room of the jail we soon saw Yagof and another prisoner brought out. As he passed through the room, he said to us, "Oh, pity, pity! Don't wait in here." He made a sweeping gesture with his hand indicating all the men in the room. We understood what he meant, so we went outside to wait under the trees on a bench in the courtyard.

It was getting late, and the evening chill began to penetrate our lightweight daytime clothing. Nevart and

I decided that we could not wait longer because of the cold and the approaching darkness. We stood up to leave, but just then a boy came running from the building.

"Don't go away!" the boy called out. "The supervisor wants to talk to you."

We saw an elderly Armenian gentleman walking along the street, so we asked him if he would stay there with us for a little while. His presence would keep passersby from getting wrong ideas about the motives of two young women loitering on the street.

Finally the shoemaker came from the building. "Good news!" he announced. "Yagof Egitkhanoff will be released. He is picking up his blankets and other things, and he will be along soon." He motioned toward the street. "But you must not wait here longer, young ladies. Permit me to accompany you home."

We thanked our elderly Armenian friend for his kindness and walked home with the Turkish gentleman.

Before long Yagof came along with the roll of bedding on his shoulder and a big smile on his face. "Well, I'm out of jail again—temporarily. Now we'd better hurry and get married before they pick me up again!"

At that moment I was too exhausted to think about anything but a good night's sleep. All day long I had walked the streets, climbed stairs, spent frustrating hours in various offices, and confronted one obstacle after another. After a nourishing supper and a relaxed visit with Yagof I went with Nevart to her home to spend the night with her.

The next day Yagof went off to the school. But at the end of the day he came home deathly ill. A severe attack of malaria, doubtless triggered by the cold night in jail, struck him down. His fever raged all that night, and he moaned over and over a prayer that he might die. All night long I ministered to his needs with cold water, lemon salts, and soda. By morning he felt better, and in a few days he was back to normal.

With Yagof well, the countdown toward a wedding resumed at an increased tempo. One serious obstacle still blocked the way: No clergyman could be found willing to perform the ceremony. Pastor Agasian would administer the rites, but his pastorate was in a different area. In order to officiate in Konya he would have to secure permission from the local Protestant bishop, the Reverend Ashjian. But Bishop Ashjian refused to grant permission until he could personally interview Yagof.

Armenian friends urged us to have a simple civil ceremony in order to avoid further dangerous delay, but both Yagof and I wanted a religious wedding.

"Why don't you get a priest of the Armenian mother church to perform the wedding?" Gregor Bodourian urged. "Father Gold of Ismit is here in exile. He could arrange matters quickly. His authority is not limited to any locality. I am sure he would be most happy to oblige. He could hold the service right here in this room."

Yagof and I still wanted a church wedding. However, I still was not certain that I should marry at this time. My mind was in such turmoil.

At last I agreed. We would be married on Sunday, October 7, 1917, in our one-room house. But one vexing question still remained: Who would perform the ceremony?

An Unusual Ceremony

One week to go—and no minister under appointment? Something had to be done quickly.

Yagof called on Pastor Agasian, and they invited Gabriel Pirenian in for a conference. The three men faced the facts and came to the only possible solution: Father Gold would have to perform a ceremony in the traditional style of the Armenian mother church, including the use of a ceremonial cross and all the other trappings of such a service. When the old priest received the invitation, he readily agreed to conduct the wedding. He would have the religious symbols taken to our house for a late afternoon service, he promised.

Oral invitations went out to a number of our immediate friends. As usual, the length of the prospective guest list grew longer as we kept thinking of other names that should be added. We intended to keep the group as small as possible in order to hold down expenses.

After the morning services in the Protestant church, Yagof went with Greg Bodourian to the Khachadouroffs. Nevart Azarian, Hysmig Shekerjian, and some of my other girl friends came home with Mother and me for lunch. They would spend the afternoon helping me get ready for the eventful evening.

Friendly neighbors helped Gregor Bodourian arrange planks on boxes as seats for the guests. The women helped Mother decorate the house with such flowers and greenery that were available in autumn.

Greg Bodourian went to the home of Father Gold to accompany him to our house. The old priest was not at home. He had gone to christen a baby on the other side of town, but he had left word that he would be at our house in time for the wedding.

"If that old priest does not show up," sputtered Greg as he told Yagof and the Khachadouroffs of this development, "I'll go and find someone else. This affair must come off before anything else happens!"

"Never mind, Greg," Mr. Khachadouroff soothed. "Let's just wait patiently. The priest will probably keep his promise."

Yagof and his friends came to the house in the middle of the afternoon. They looked apprehensively at the growing crowd overflowing the room into the yard. Word had gone from mouth to mouth, and friends were arriving from all over town. Yagof hurried off to buy additional food for the unexpected number of guests.

The time set for the ceremony approached. Mrs. Bodourian and Nevart began to help me dress. We used the sun porch as a bridal chamber. They had borrowed a bride's coronet of waxed orange blossoms and a veil. They put my long hair up in a braid and arranged it tastefully on top of my head. With my white graduation dress lengthened to floor length, and with a bridal bouquet, I was ready to make my appearance.

The groom had a tailor-made gray suit. This suit, made for him before his exile from Erzurum, had reached him miraculously. I will not relate that story here. At any rate, we both wore attractive clothes that a kind Providence had provided.

The two bridesmaids, Nevart and Hysmig, wore

white silk blouses and long black skirts. The two groomsmen, Garo Khachadouroff and Gregor Bodourian, wore suits of good quality. So the whole party of exiled young people put on a brave appearance. I can assure you that all of us suffered qualms of conscience as we thought of the thousands of our less fortunate countrymen suffering unmentionable privation.

Yagof had fared worse than the rest of us. He had witnessed horrors beyond our imagination, and he had so recently felt the fury of human hatred that he had restlessly paced in and out of the sun porch as the women arranged the bridal costume. In one outburst of the agony in his mind he blurted out, "How can you have the heart to be adorned like that, my love?"

Mrs. Khachadouroff gently took Yagof's arm. "Please, my dear Baron Hagop, don't worry. We must make the most of this joyful occasion." She led him to the door into the main room. "You just wait there in the house. It is almost time for the ceremony."

As if right on cue, the big street gate opened, and the priest, decked in his clerical robe, entered. Garo followed, carrying the ceremonial cross.

One of the men quickly placed an ornamented chair in one corner at the front of the room. Someone—I'm not sure who—led me in and seated me on the chair; the two bridesmaids stood one on each side of me. The groom and Greg came to the front and stood in the other corner. Then the priest and Garo entered the room. Everyone stood to greet the priest; he acknowledged the greeting with words of blessing, and the guests sat down again. A seemingly interminable ceremony got underway.

Another minor miracle occurred at this point. Yagof and I had wished that someone from Erzurum, his hometown, could somehow witness this ceremony.

But we did not know of anyone here who had survived the dreadful evacuation of that unhappy city. As the priest questioned Yagof and then me as to birthplace, parents, and so forth, guests continued to arrive.

Suddenly Yagof gasped. "It's the Khulbegians," he whispered as he saw a man and a woman enter. "He was a teacher in Erzurum!" Yagof could hardly contain his excitement.

Having completed the recording of necessary information for the marriage certificate, the priest turned toward the guests. He spent a few minutes in conversing informally with the people. Then he stood up for the ceremony, and we all stood also.

Barour, Garo's thirteen-year-old brother, and Father Gold's young son of about the same age each held a large candle and stood one on each side of the priest. The candles were lighted, and then the priest motioned for Yagof and me to come from our corners. He took my right hand and placed it in Yagof's hand. Garo, holding the cross, stood by Yagof and Mrs. Khachadouroff stood by me. Then Father Gold began reading the wedding ceremony.

That particular Sunday had been a beautiful day, with bright sunlight bathing the landscape after a long cold spell. Now, in the late afternoon, what had been welcome warmth throughout the day became oppressive heat in that packed room. The heat generated by many bodies in close quarters made the atmosphere almost unbearable. A large kerosene lamp hanging almost directly over our heads added to the discomfort. Poor Yagof, already perspiring earlier from nervousness, now had sweat pouring down his face. He had to mop his brow repeatedly. Even I and the other women had to dab furtively at a trickle from time to time.

Father Gold droned on and on. I thought my legs would collapse under me before he would finish. He had

Yagof and me return to our corners; then he called us together again. He had us hold hands; then he had us stand side by side. He read the duties of the husband; he read the duties of the wife. On and on and on—

My mind wandered. I began to think, as I so often did, of the desperate condition of my people. Why should I be privileged to stand here when so many loved ones and friends suffered in far away places. Tears began to roll down my face.

Yagof, seeing the tears, turned ever so slightly toward me and whispered, "Marichen, what is it?"

I could not answer.

Garo waved the cross close to our heads like a fan to stir a bit of a breeze through our hair.

Father Gold broke through our reverie with the solemn questions, first to the groom, and then to me, "Do you, Baron Hagop Egitkhanoff, take this woman . . . until death do you part? . . . Do you, Mary Abelian, take this man . . . until death do you part?" We both stated firmly, "I do."

Then the priest surprised us. From somewhere he produced a long cord made of shining strands of blue and white twisted together. This he placed around Yagof's neck and then around mine and tied us together.

But even now more ceremonies had to be performed. Yagof and I both kissed the priest's hands. We each took a sip from the cup the priest held out to us. Yagof kissed the cross. We both kissed the hands of our godfather and godmother, the Khachadouroffs. Then Father Gold introduced Baron and Mrs. Egitkhanoff and invited our guests to come forward to congratulate and kiss the bride and groom.

Quickly Mrs. Khachadouroff cleared people from the center of the room. Having no table big enough, she simply spread a large tablecloth on the floor, picnic style, and placed the food on it. She had anticipated the crowd and had brought a good amount of macaroni and a big dish of roasted meat. She also had made a large batch of *chöreg* (sweet bread). Her provisions, added to what Yagof had purchased, made an ample supply.

There was great joy in that room for a little while. Dear friends tried to forget the circumstances of our being in such a place, and pleasantries and laughter prevailed. Another pleasant surprise concerned an old man who had been a master tailor in Bardezag, my hometown, for many years. It turned out that he was a native of Erzurum, Yagof's hometown—and a brother-in-law of Yagof's uncle! This old man brought along a violin and played a number of Armenian folk songs to enliven the feast. Everyone agreed that it was a very lovely afternoon.

One amazing aspect of the afternoon's affair was that Turkish authorities did not interfere. Either they did not know what was happening, or else they deliberately closed their eyes. We had no indication that any Turks except our landlord's family knew of the gathering.

At any rate, a very weary Mrs. Egitkhanoff and an almost exhausted Baron Lucky collapsed for the night on the *sederlik* in that Turkish guesthouse. The honeymoon would have to come later.

The next day Yagof hired a carriage to take the two of us to the little Greek hill town of Sillé a few miles northwest of Konya. There we stayed with friends for a few glorious days. On the roof of their house they had a guest room which became our honeymoon cottage.

All too soon we had to return to Konya, Yagof to his teaching and I to my new role as a housewife. Yagof could not risk the consequences of a long absence from his job.

Good News

Marriage solved one set of problems; but Yagof and I, as well as all of my loved ones in Konya, were still displaced persons living under constant uncertainty about governmental attitude towards us. Our most pressing immediate concern was to find a source of income. Yagof had to work without pay at the technical school in order to escape arrest and deportation. We hoped that this arrangement would change before long.

One day as Yagof walked home from work, he passed through the big covered market. He noticed a man following him and apparently trying to get a good view of his face. A chill of suspicion caused Yagof to quicken his steps; the man could be a secret police or some enemy intent on an evil mission.

The man overtook Yagof and placed a hand on his shoulder. "Don't run away from me, young man," he said. "I have good news for you."

Yagof wondered if this was some kind of trick to take him into custody. Good news? Would it be that he was to be sent to Beysehir?

"Do you have a sister in Mosul?" the man asked.

"No sir," Yagof answered. I have no living family." He wiped the nervous perspiration from his forehead. "I am alone."

"But there is a lady in Mosul who looks exactly like you." The older man studied Yagof's face again and noticed the agitation. "Don't be afraid, young man. I'm telling the truth. I was in exile there, and I am here with permission to visit my brother, the Reverend Ashjian. My name is Moses Ashjian.

"As far as I know," Yagof insisted, "no one from my family survived."

"But that lady must be your sister. Where are you from? I should add that the lady has a little girl and two small boys with her. She earns a living by sewing."

Could it be? Yagof knew that his sister had taken lessons in sewing. She had three children, a girl and two boys. Maybe she and her children had escaped the general massacre.

"Sir—" Yagof could hardly speak because of the emotions surging through his body. "Sir, we were deported from Erzurum. My sister Shoushan with her children left the city with the same caravan in which I was forced to travel. But our cruel guards drove us apart. I supposed that those dear ones perished with the hundreds of others along the way. They were not among the few surviviors who arrived in Aleppo with me."

"I am sure that this woman is your sister," the old man said. "She also was from Erzurum. She lived near the place where I stayed in Mosul. She did some sewing for me. In fact, she made this necktie I'm wearing. I know her well. I believe her given name is Shoushan." He turned as if to leave.

Yagof reached for the man's hand. "You must come home with me!" he urged. "I can't let you go without hearing more and sharing the news with my wife."

The first I knew about this encounter was when I saw the big gate open and Yagof and the other man enter hand in hand. "Oh, Yagof, had been arrested again," I thought, "and they are coming to get me!"

But Yagof wore a big smile. He waved and called out, "Marichen, don't be afraid. There is news—good news!"

What a session followed. The two men talked about the unbelievable experiences they had been through. We all wept together and praised the Lord together.

"We all love your sister," the man said. "She is an honorable woman. She never sold herself to save her life as many women did, God pity them. She never stayed in an Arab's house. She preserved her dignity and worked for a living. We love her children too, especially little Levon."

"Levon!" Yagof caught his breath and the color drained from his face. "Levon! Then my mother must be there too, because Levon is my baby brother!"

The old man shook his head.

"Is the other boy's name Kegam?" Yagof asked leaning forward in the earnestness of his inquiry. "My sister's daughter is named Knarig, and her boys are Khajag and Vasken. How is it that Levon and Kegam are living with that family?"

"I'm sorry that I don't know," Moses Ashjian answered. "I supposed that Levon and Kegam were her own sons." He registered obvious regret. "Listen," he said. "Why don't I write a letter to her and enclose a picture of yourself, Yagof? Then if she is your sister, she can write to you and answer all the questions I can't."

Many weeks later a letter came from Shoushan. She told us that the small boys were her brothers, her baby brothers—Yagof's brothers. Shoushan could not believe that Yagof had survived the death march. She had watched horrified as her husband and hundreds of other men were brutally murdered. Her own little boys and her mother had perished under the merciless treatment which she and her daughter had somehow endured.

One morning about three weeks after our wedding the superintendent of the Turkish technical school called Yagof to his office. First he praised Yagof's good work and expressed his pleasure in having such a skillful teacher. Then he said, "Yagof, you may now work only half a day here and have the rest of the day to do some other work so you can earn a living."

Well, this was not exactly what Yagof had expected, but it was certainly better than working full time for nothing. He could now be free to seek a means of providing an income.

Yagof had one particular skill—making uppers for shoes. For employing that skill he needed a shoemaker's sewing machine, and had no money with which to purchase such a machine. But "man's extremity is God's opportunity." Again a kind Providence intervened in our affairs and sent help from unexpected quarters.

Mehmed, our Kurd (Armenian) friend, learning of our need, offered to lend us money for the purchase. We didn't even surmise that the young man had money. So we happily purchased the machine, and Yagof set up shop on our sun porch. A few weeks later he found a small stall available in the big covered market and moved his shop there. He found a ready sale for his products, and our financial situation improved.

As a chilly fall merged into an early cold winter, we listened to circulating rumors and wondered what the future held. Something seemed to be happening to the Turkish forces, but we were not sure what. The British, it seemed, had invaded Palestine after gaining naval control of the eastern Mediterranean. What would this mean for Onnig Pirenian in Jerusalem? Some reports in November even insisted that Gaza was already in British hands. And among the rumors from the battlefront, the hope of a soon return of exiles to their homes persisted. But to us in Konya these words on the winds seemed unreal. We knew that our kinsmen were still suffering and dying in far-off places. We, in Konya, fought off recurrent attacks of malaria and carried on the daily struggle to provide ourselves with necessary food.

December brought exceptionally heavy snow. People had to shovel the snow from their flat roofs, Turkish houses not being constructed to support the weight of the snow. In our house Yagof was down with a severe attack of fever, so Mother and I climbed to the roof and managed to remove the snow. That exertion put us in bed just as Yagof recovered from his bout.

Even in exile we could not allow the new year to begin without notice. We spent New Year's Eve with the Khachadouroffs in a traditional celebration. We hoped that this year 1918 would bring better times.

January wore on in the familiar routine, and February seemed to offer no change—until February 19.

A Turkish messenger boy came running to our house with a personal note. I ripped open the envelope and stared at the contents in disbelief. It was from Onnig Pirenian at the Konya railroad station. Onnig was on his way home. He wanted us to get his brother Gabriel and come to the station for a visit. We lost no time in complying with that request.

What a joyful reunion. Mother held Onnig's hand and, with tears coursing down her face, begged him to stay with us for a while.

"No, Mother," he said, "it is impossible. I am still under army orders, and I must go on my way."

Onnig explained what had happened. When Jerusalem fell to the British on December 9, the Turkish officers offered to let Onnig go free to remain with the Christian conquerors; in fact, they had urged him to do so for his own safety. but he chose to stay with his own country's forces as a loyal citizen. So now he was receiving preferential treatment. On this train he had charge of a special mission to bottle mineral water from springs in the interior of Anatolia and ship it back to the army hospitals. He would be allowed to remain in Eskisehir with his wife after completing his mission and be assigned to military duties in his own city. His years of faithful Christian service had won the respect of his Muslim superiors.

Onnig had news from many relatives and friends he had seen in Palestine and Syria—most of them sad derelicts of humanity who had held onto the fragile thread of life under extreme hardships. At one place he found my cousin Garabed Abelian and his family. They had subsisted on grass for two weeks. Onnig could not tell us all the news, because his train was due to leave, and we had to let him go.

March 4, 1918. The Turkish citizens of Konya went wild with jubilation. The new Russian regime had made a separate truce agreement with Turkey; thus forces guarding against a Russian invasion could be sent to other zones. The celebration lasted all day and on throughout most of the night. We hardly felt like joining in the festivities, because we did not know how the new arrangements would affect us. If Yagof would now be sent to Russia, I would have to go with him. What would happen to Mother in that event? On the other hand, the Turkish government might now feel free to exile all Armenians with Russian citizenship. Our future depended entirely on the caprice of government officials.

Days passed with no word of any change in our condition. We tried not to worry about a situation we could not change. We carried on the familiar routine as cheerfully as possible—Yagof at his schoolteaching and at his trade, I with my household duties and my language lessons. Fellowship with my Armenian friends and Yagof's Russian friends helped pass the time. Weekly Sabbath services, usually in our home, and Sunday services in the Protestant church fed us spiritually.

Finally, about the first of April, orders came from the capital that all Russian subjects would be returned from exile. Turkish Armenians would be released soon afterward. We were required to register with the local authorities and state the destination to which we wished to be sent. Good news! Yes, but with a sad twist.

First of all no Russian Armenians could return to the Armenian heartland—Erzurum, Kars, or other cities in areas still disputed with the Russians and adjacent to the newly formed Soviet Republic of Armenia. They might be allowed into the Russian republic later on when conditions stabilized, but no one knew when that would be. So Yagof could not choose his hometown.

On the other hand, I could not choose Bardezag, my hometown, because I was no longer an Abelian and had no claim to any of my family's property there.

About the only choice open to us was Istanbul. As far as I was concerned, that city offered definite advantages. I had a large circle of friends there, and the headquarters of the Seventh-day Adventist work in Turkey was there. We registered to be sent to Istanbul.

Then we waited. And waited.

The Waiting Game

One afternoon toward the middle of June Gabriel Pirenian stopped by the marketplace for a brief visit with Yagof. As the two of them chatted pleasantly, they heard gunshots on the street, and soon several police officers ran into the building. They dashed about among the little stalls, obviously looking for someone.

Suddenly one of the officers spotted Gabriel standing in Yagof's stall.

"Here he is!" the policeman shouted, and the others converged on the scene.

"Aha!" one of the officers exclaimed. "You are Reuben Kouyoumjian, aren't you?" He grabbed Gabriel's arm. "You thought you could escape!"

"Oh, no, sir," Gabriel said. "My name is Pirenian." He took from his pocket the identification paper he carried and showed it to the officer.

The officers, not willing to admit their error in identifying the fugitive, hustled Gabriel off to jail.

Mother and Yagof and I went to the police and managed to arrange bail for Gabriel's release for the night. We went with him to his home.

"Oh, Ebross Mairig," Gabriel sobbed, "you will take care of my children, won't you? They love you as their own grandmother."

Gabriel's wife had died in childbirth during the previous winter, the child having died also. His seventeen-year-old daughter Azniv had been a mother to three younger children, the youngest only four years old.

"Of course I will take care of them, Gabriel," Mother assured him. "But don't give up hope. We'll try to get you released."

The next afternoon we went to Gabriel's home again and joined him in a season of prayer and Bible reading. Gabriel was reading Psalm 130—"Out of the depths have I cried unto thee, O Lord. Lord, hear my voice." He had not finished the psalm when officers came to take him off to jail.

Early the next morning Mother and Azniv went everywhere they could think of in search of help to have Gabriel released. Yagof and I spent as much time as possible in the same fruitless endeavor. Friends joined us in prayer for Gabriel.

Mother Makrouhi Boghosian and my mother prepared a bundle and took it to Gabriel in jail. The officers questioned them about Gabriel's identity and wanted some more witnesses. So Mother Makrouhi sent for Papa Paul and a well-known man from Bardezag, a Mr. Artin Kurkjian.

The officers questioned the two men closely. Of course they both testified that the prisoner was their friend Gabriel Pirenian.

"Gabriel Pirenian?" the chief questioned. "Are you sure?"

"Oh, yes," Papa Paul said. "We know him well."

"Look at this." The officer held out the identification paper Gabriel had carried at the time of his arrest. "The name here is Megerdich Pirenian."

Both men stared at the paper, amazement written on their faces.

"But—I'm sure—. There must be some mistake," Artin Kurkjain stammered.

"That's right," the chief agreed. "That is all gentlemen. You may leave now."

Gabriel had made the human error of trying to escape military service in order to stay with his motherless children. He was carrying the birth certificate of his oldest brother, already deceased. The age attested by the certificate would place him beyond draft age. But he had not told his friends of this ruse; therefore Papa Paul and Artin Kurkjain were caught off guard. I do not know whether or not they would have testified to a falsehood. At any rate, Gabriel was sent off to join thousands of other unfortunate men.

A few days later we received a letter from Eskisehir. It was from Gabriel. He had been placed on a train headed toward Istanbul rather than toward Syria. At Eskisehir, when the train stopped, Gabriel noticed guards standing on the station platform, on either side of the entrance to the car in which he rode. These guards, he knew, were waiting for him. There was nothing to do but leave the train. Gabriel stepped off the train, but the guards seemed not to see him. He walked past them. Then he remembered he had left his luggage on the train. Now, what should he do?

Gabriel turned. The guards still stood at their posts of duty. They appeared oblivious to their surroundings. Gabriel walked back between the guards and onto the train where he retrieved his luggage. Then, once more he walked off that train, past the guards, who didn't notice him, and off to his brother's home.

We sighed a sigh of relief when we read his letter. Surely the God of heaven had blinded the guards and protected Gabriel that day.

Just before Gabriel had had his trouble with the law,

my sister Heripsime and I spent several hours one day filling out various papers in preparation for returning from exile. Heripsime had to establish her relation to Mother. Of course, I was the wife of a Russian citizen, so my case was settled; but I helped my sister. In our conversation with the officers I happened to mention that I had worked in Herr Mauer's home.

"Get a statement to that effect from Herr Mauer," one of the officers ordered. "If he agrees with your story, I'll believe you."

So in the heat of the day my sister and I walked to the German quarters near the railroad station.

"What if Herr Mauer is not here?" Heripsime asked weakly.

"I don't know," I answered. "Maybe a statement from Elsie or Sister Clara will do."

But another evidence of our good Lord's tender care awaited us. Herr Mauer was at home!

"Well, Mary!" the jovial official exclaimed. "What brings you here?"

I explained our errand.

"Why, sure!" He looked at the paper I carried from the office. "Here. I'll write a statement for you." He sat at a small desk near the door and wrote a few words. Then he handed the paper back to me. I read his statement: "I know Mary Egitkhanoff very well. I also know her mother and her sister and four children, all of them now living in Konya."

We thanked Herr Mauer profusely and started back toward the city hall. Now our steps seemed lighter and our hearts sang for joy.

"Mary," Heripsime almost sang, "that signature under that statement is worth more than five gold liras!"

Still we waited for governmental wheels to turn.

Mother wore herself sick taking care of Gabriel's

four children. The two oldest—Azniv, seventeen, and Jedediah about two years younger—could have been a real help. Instead they constantly bickered about who should carry the water or do other household chores. To keep peace Mother usually did the work herself. She also had to stand in line several hours every day for the bread ration.

One day Mrs. Khachadouroff visited us. She urged us to move from the Turkish section to the Greek quarter where she lived. She had heard from reliable sources that it was dangerous for Russian people to live in a Turkish neighborhood. She said she knew of a small room available near her place. We thanked her for her concern, but we did not move at once. After all, weren't we all going to leave town soon?

Unstable conditions in Turkey caused endless confusion and delay. The old sultan died early in July, and most of his top officials fled to Germany to save their lives. Opposition to the ruling party spread throughout the country. We heard stories of fires raging in Istanbul. Some said the fires were set by Armenian and German agents; others pretended to know that Allied airplanes had dropped fire bombs. Orders came to withhold all provisions from German soldiers, thus forcing them to return to Germany.

All we knew in Konya was that we must simply wait and hope.

July and August dragged by. Shortages of everything sent prices soaring. Landlords raised the rent to keep pace with the general inflation. Then our Turkish landlord's wife served notice that we must move out. Her husband, soon to be released from the army because of his age, would be coming home and they would need our guesthouse for friends.

Yagof and I decided to move into the small room near the Khachadouroffs, which was still available.

The Return

During the month of September 1918 the British and their allies pushed north from Jerusalem and took Megiddo, then Damascus, and finally Alleppo. Although we in Konya did not have specific details, everyone seemed sure that Turkey could not maintain effective resistance much longer. Internal affairs had reached deplorable disorganization. The old sultan, Mohammed V had died in July, and the new sultan seemed unable to keep the government functioning properly.

Repeatedly we heard that exiles would be allowed to return to their homes, but the necessary orders did not come through. Over and over our hopes were dashed.

Suddenly, about the middle of October, Yagof and I, along with other Russian citizens, received official permission to leave as soon as space was available on a train. Now we faced the necessity of deciding what to do about my dear mother. She could not go with me, because she was a Turkish citizen and I was married to a Russian citizen. We could not go away and leave her alone with Gabriel's four children. Such a separation would tear our hearts out.

Some Turkish Armenians were being allowed to leave Konya under certain circumstances. Yagof and

I, in consultation with my sister Heripsime, decided that we should apply for permission to let Mother and the four children accompany us as far as Eskisehir. There Mother could be with my older sister Varsenig, and Gabriel could arrange for his children.

I spent a whole week going from one office to another in a vain attempt to secure the necessary papers. Everywhere I met the same rebuff: "Only officers and their families are receiving permission now." But over and over I saw women called out of line behind me to receive the papers we all wanted. And every evening I told Mother and Yagof the discouraging results.

"I will not go back to those officers again." I announced one morning.

"Just one more day, Marichen." Yagof drew me to him and tilted my down cast face up to look into my eyes. "We can't leave Mama here with the children, can we?"

I closed my eyes and tried to pull away.

"You love them more than I do, don't you, deary?" he asked in a gentle tone of voice. "What if something should happen to Azniv?" He paused and held me even closer. "You know what I mean, don't you? The guilt of leaving her here unprotected would torment us forever."

"But, Yagof," I wailed, "There is no use in going." Tears coursed down my cheeks. "They won't pay any attention to me."

Then he proposed a plan that I could not accept. He knew one of the officers quite well; in fact, he and the officer had met more than once at a cafe near the government building and had sat together over lunch. "Here," he said, handing me a couple of low-denomination paper bills, "give these to that officer with greetings from me. Just tell him that this is a small reminder of our friendship and an invitation for him to have some coffee at my expense."

"Yagof," I was shocked almost beyond words. "I—that is—I could never do that!"

"Now, now, deary!" Yagof remained calm. "That little bit of money is not a bribe. It is only a gift for a friend."

"But I can't do it!" I stamped my foot for emphasis.

"But you promised to obey your husband."

"Not to do wrong!"

This was our first major argument. And Yagof won! I had to admit that there seemed to be no other course of action.

I think I must have looked guilty as I walked up to the officer's desk. I felt utterly miserable. "*Effendy*," I said quietly so that no one else would hear, "my husband, Yagof Egitkhanoff, wishes to remind you of his friendship." I slipped the bank notes under the man's hands.

The officer jerked his hand up in a startled gesture. "You dare to offer a bribe right in a government office?" he shouted. "That is a capital offense. You should be sent to the gallows!" And he took me by the arm, propelling me into the War Department Court of Justice.

A row of judges sat behind a high desk, and I stood quaking in front of them. For a moment panic seized me as I realized that this tribunal could sentence me to be hanged with no appeal. Almost at once the fear subsided and I felt a power sustaining me. Words of Scripture came to my mind without conscious effort to recall them. "Ye shall be brought before governors and kings for my sake, for a testimony against them and the Gentiles. But when they deliver you up, take no thought how or what ye shall speak: for it shall be given you in that same hour what ye shall speak." Matthew 10:18,19. "Be ready always to give an answer to every man that asketh you a reason of the hope that is in you with meekness and fear: having a good conscience." 1 Peter 3:15, 16. My mind pictured Daniel calmly facing the hungry lions, and suddenly the judges no longer appeared fierce. I thought I even detected a sympathetic attitude behind their stern appearance.

"What is this that you have done, young lady?" the chief judge asked. "Do you know the penalty for bribing a government official?"

"My lords, honorable judges, it is wrong to give a bribe." I spoke with all the conviction I could muster. "I fear God, as you do, and I know God's penalty for sin." Then I went on to explain the circumstances. I had obeyed my husband in offering a gift of friendship to this officer in the hope that his favor could accomplish for me what a week of fruitless effort had failed to produce. I dwelt at some length on my crippled mother's care for the four motherless children. I closed my defense with reference to my clear conscience which would allow me to stand unashamed before the judgment bar of Christ, our resurrected Lord, when He will judge all nations.

The judges conferred together for several minutes while I stood before the bench with bowed head awaiting their decision. They called up the officer who had condemned me and talked with him quietly for quite a while.

As the group separated to return to their positions, I heard one man say, "She is a God-fearing woman, no doubt. Justice must be done to her and others like her."

"Your life is granted to you, gentle lady," the chief judge intoned. "You are free!"

"Allah be with you," the other judges said in unison.

Then the chief judge instructed the officer to prepare the necessary papers for Mother and the four children's immediate passage to Eskisehir—even before Yagof and I could leave.

A few days later we joyfully put my precious mother and her charges on the train. The Lord had worked things out better than we had hoped.

On October 30, 1918, the Turkish provisional government signed a capitulation to the victorious Allies. The war had finally ended. Now the railroad trains were more crowded than ever with demobilized troops returning from the front. Exiles waiting for transportation had to be ready on short notice to take any available space.

Our friends the Khachadouroffs wanted very much for Yagof and me to travel with them, and fortunately it worked out that way. We received notice on Monday, November 4, to go to the railroad station. What a mess of displaced humanity waited for transportation—Russians, Germans, Armenians, Turks, and others.

Finally at about four o'clock in the afternoon the Russians received orders to board. The reality of freedom almost overwhelmed me.

Early the next morning the train stopped at Afyon. How different the fields around the city looked now. No makeshift tents. No mounted guards herding miserable crowds into cattle cars. No clouds of dust rising from the road where starving marchers trudged endlessly toward oblivion. Now the empty fields looked almost pleasant.

The Khachadouroffs and another Russian family left the train at Afyon to go west to Smyrna. We proceeded north to Eskisehir.

Mother met the train in Eskisehir the next evening. Varsenig and Onnig were both sick at the time, but they welcomed us to their little two-room cottage. With Gabriel and his four children staying there, Yagof and I brought to ten the number of people to bed down at night. Even so, we had to stay several days for the sheer joy of being together again.

On Sabbath a small group of Adventists met at the Pirenian home. Onnig conducted a morning and an afternoon service. A picnic lunch spread under the trees a short distance in the country gave us sweet fellowship with other returned exiles. It was a blessed experience.

After four glorious days with other loved ones, Yagof and I took Mother and boarded the train again. We arranged our passage with a stopover in Izmit. We planned to leave Mother in Bardezag, the old hometown, to take possession again of our family holdings there. Yagof and I would go on to Istanbul.

At Izmit we found that an important bundle of our baggage—our bedding—had not been put off the train. Fortunately we found friends who arranged for us to stay in the parish house of one of the churches. We stayed there two nights while we took care of the legal papers for Mother's repossession of the Bardeszag property.

What a sight the bay presented as we crossed late in the afternoon. Warships crowded the whole bay. More than seventy British, French, Italian, and Greek vessels of all sizes swung at anchor, their lights gleaming in the early dusk and casting sparkling trails across the ripples of the water.

Onnig had tried to prepare us for our arrival at Bardezag, but his words had failed to portray the devastation. The utter ruin of our beloved town almost overwhelmed us. All along the waterfront stood vacant and broken buildings. The pier where busy ships had docked now lay broken and in ruins. No carriages with cheerful drivers waited to carry passengers from the steamship up to town. The littered streets seemed to be deserted.

Yagof and I left Mother and another woman with their belongings in a large house which had been made into a hay barn. We would spend the night there too, but first we wanted to walk farther into town despite the gathering darkness. Three young men, an Armenian and two Turkish officers, walked with us.

Oh, the sad sights that brought uncontrollable tears to my eyes. Ruined vineyards where century-old vines had been chopped down for firewood. Rich garden plots grown up to weeds and littered with debris. Mulberry groves, whose leaves had been used for silkworm culture, had been chopped down and burned. The external timbers of many of the homes had been ripped off and used for firewood. Other homes had been reduced to piles of rubble.

It was dark when we reached the marketplace. Adjoining the marketplace stood what had been the beautiful Armenian church. Now we could hardly make our way through the ruins.

A little distance beyond the church we found the family of dear friends in a partially renovated house. They invited us to share the shelter of their home, and we gladly accepted. We returned to the waterfront hay barn and brought the two older women through the town. Then we spent almost the whole night talking of the life we had shared before the exile—a life now gone beyond recall.

Early the next morning Mother and Yagof and I set out on our mission to see for ourselves the state of the house we had locked up only a little more than three years before. My mind carried the picture of that spacious house surrounded by the well-kept grounds and stone-paved walks. Onnig had told us, but I could not visualize what had happened.

Nothing looked the same. Only familiarity with distances from one point to another could indicate where we were going. Around a corner, over a little rise, and the house should stand just ahead. But nothing—only a hole in the ground surrounded by scattered stones. The house had been taken apart piece by piece, the timbers carried off for the use in constructing a drab barracks for soldiers on the nearby campus of the Armenian school.

Finally we turned and walked on up the street. We turned the corner and saw the homes of my two uncles still more or less intact. Beyond the little creek stood the homes of my cousins, also in fair condition. Mother could claim all five homes, because all of those families had perished in the death march. But what could Mother do with five homes? She would need only a small place.

Home at last. We left Mother and my aunt comfortably settled in a room with a view of the hills behind Bardezag in one direction and a vista of the bay in the other direction. There they would stay until the family in one of the houses mother had chosen to live in could move out.

Uneasy Peace

Istanbul. The beautiful city of Turkey—ancient Byzantium of Greek and Roman times, beloved center of Constantine's empire renamed Constantinople, and then later, Istanbul. This cosmopolitan city controlling the Bosporus entrance to the Black Sea had been the prize in wars from the dawn of history, through the collapse of Rome, past the Crusades in medieval times, and into the twentieth century. Yagof and I arrived by steamship on a very rainy November 20, 1918.

Our first duty in Istanbul was to have our Russian passports validated by registering at the Russian Consulate. Elder Erzberger, the newly appointed head of the Seventh-day Adventist mission, testified for us to satisfy officials that Yagof's claim to citizenship was genuine. We were then given a room in the Russian hospital as temporary quarters.

Early on a Monday morning not long after our arrival, a noise on the hospital grounds awakened us. There was a slam of automobile doors and the sound of heavy boots on the pavement. Almost at once we heard loud banging on our door that threatened to break the door in.

Yagof quickly jerked on his trousers and then opened the door. Eight Turkish, two French, and two Italian officers pushed their way into the room. The Turkish officers in charge commanded Yagof to get dressed and follow them. Two officers grabbed his arms and roughly shoved him to a chair to put on his shoes.

Yagof could not speak. Who knows what thoughts flooded his mind?

I found my voice. "Gentlemen." I quavered, "What is the reason for this arrest?"

Two or three of the officers muttered something about a list of Bolshevist activists who were being rounded up.

"But Yagof Egitkhanoff is not one of them," I protested. "He is sick, but if he must go, tell me where he will be taken, I must know."

The two officers jerked Yagof to his feet. All this time he had not said a word, only uttering groans with each breath.

I was terrified. Had someone betrayed him as an escaped exile? I wondered. Would he now be sent to prison or worse? Then I remembered a word one of the men had said: *list*. "Let me see that list," I demanded. The officer in charge held out a piece of paper, which I examined carefully.

"There is no Yagof Egitkhanoff on this list," I said as forcefully as I could. "The instructions here are written in English. Can any of you speak English?"

Another officer took the list and looked at it. "Stay here, men," he said in Turkish and then repeated the orders in French. "Don't let him get away. I'm going to see about this list." He stalked out of the room and slammed the door.

Soon the officer returned with the hospital administrator, a friendly Russian.

"I'm sorry, gentlemen," the big Russian said in Turkish. "This man has never had his name on a list of suspects.'' He put a hand on Yagof's shoulder. Yagof Egitkhanoff is one of the finest men I know.''

The officer in charge motioned to the two holding Yagof's arms. They released their iron grip. The officer jerked his head toward the door, and one by one the men filed out. The officer paused in the door and spoke to us. ''Sorry for the mistake,'' he said. He turned abruptly and disappeared into the hallway.

Meanwhile other parties of raiders had combed other parts of the hospital. Soon we heard boots on the pavement again; and, looking out the window, we could see in the dim morning light, a number of men in chains being shoved into the police cars. How Yagof and I praised the Lord for this deliverance!

As the year neared its end, Yagof became restless without specific employment. He decided to visit my mother in Bardezag. He had fallen in love with that beautiful country— despite the devastated town—on his first visit there. Also we wanted to be sure that Mother was getting along all right. I was not well enough to make the trip, so he went alone. A teenage girl friend came to stay with me while my husband was gone.

During Yagof's absence some of my friends began to talk to me about my marriage with someone not of my faith. Of course, I explained the circumstances, and they agreed that I had been placed in an inescapable trap. But even so, I wondered if God had forgiven me for violating my conscience. This had always bothered me—marrying one not a Seventh-day Adventist.

We had a season of prayer together as the minutes ticked away toward midnight. ''Dear Lord,'' I prayed, ''forgive me for being presumptious and asking for a sign, but if I have been forgiven, let my husband return from his visit with a decision to follow his Saviour in baptism and a life of obedience."

Imagine my joy a few days later when Yagof returned. Almost his first words after our welcome embrace were, 'Mary, dearie, I have decided to be baptized and take an oath to live as our heavenly Father requires. Are you glad?"

Was I glad? Those words were almost a direct quotation of the sign I had requested. All I could say was, "Oh, Yagof!" I lost myself in another embrace as tears of joy flowed freely.

Serious studies with Elder Erzberger followed, and Yagof was baptized with several others on Sabbath, May 3, in the quiet waters of the Bosporus near Galata.

During the summer of 1919 Yagof and I traveled with Elder Erzberger to visit various groups of Adventists in the towns around Ismit Bay, including Adapazari, Ismit, Bardezag, and Shak-shak. Of course we had a cherished visit with my mother and found her well and happy. My sister Heripsime had returned to her home in Shak-shak. More fortunate than many other returning exiles, she found her house intact, the well still usable, the vineyard and fruit trees still growing—although quite neglected. They even had mulberry trees for their silkworm culture, and they had a garden. We spent two wonderful nights in that home embarking at Yalova for our return to Istanbul.

During the trip Yagof had looked for opportunities to find employment. In Izmit we found one of my cousins, the only son of Aunt Martha, who with his wife and children had returned from the Syrian desert. He now had a successful shoemaking business there, and he urged us to move to Izmit. Oh, how we hoped we would be able to accept his offer. We would be near Mother and others of my loved ones. We returned to Istanbul with that dream alive in our hearts.

By the end of September we had made the necessary

arrangements and moved to Izmit. We found a lonely old house standing by itself at the end of the ruins of the Armenian section of town. The house provided suitable living quarters, and there was an ever-flowing spring of fine water nearby. We considered ourselves fortunate to find such a good place in which to live. Gabriel Pirenian and his children took the downstairs part of the house.

One day late in October Yagof went to Istanbul with two other men to buy supplies of leather and other goods. They planned to return on Friday afternoon. Friday turned out to be a stormy day, and I waited until late afternoon, wondering why Yagof had not returned. Azniv, Gabriel's daughter, had spent the two nights with me and now wanted to return to her own home downstairs before the Sabbath. We spent several restless sessions standing at the upstairs windows to look for the absent husband.

Finally, when it was almost sundown, I said, "Azniv, let's go down to see if Asadour has returned." Asadour and his brother were the two men who had gone to Istanbul with Yagof. They lived in one of the Turkish houses bordering the ruins.

Together Azniv and I walked down the hill. There by his house sat Asadour with his pretty wife beside him. I almost fainted. A thousand thoughts passed through my mind about Yagof's fate.

"Oh, Mary," Asadour exclaimed "We have news for you."

"What is it?" I demanded. "Tell me quickly!"

"Oh, I forgot to tell you." A big grin covered Asadour's face. "Your husband asked me to take the news to you, but now you have been too clever for me and have come running here." He must have seen the troubled look on my face, for he added quickly, "It's good news, Mary. Your husband is all right. He'll be home in a couple of days. He ran into some important business he has to see about."

"Asadour!" I stamped my foot impatiently. "Stop playing games with me. This is no time for jokes. What happened? Please tell me."

"Well," Asadour said slowly, "he found his sister and her children—Yagof's brothers, I understand—near the railroad station."

I sat down, too weak with surprise to remain standing. "Tell me about it," I begged.

"We started from Istanbul in the morning by steamer, Asadour explained; "but a violent storm forced us back to the harbor. So we went to the railroad station to catch a train. As we turned from the ticket window, a man came up to Yagof and said, 'Do you see that boy over there in the Arabian clothes? He is your brother.' Yagof thought it was some kind of trick, but the man called the boy's name, Kegam, and the boy came to where we were talking. Of course Yagof could not recognize the boy who had changed so much over the years, but the boy easily recognized Yagof. The boy said that his sister-mother with the other children were camped with others in a field near the station. They had secured passage on an English steamer to Istanbul hoping to find Yagof there. Well, Yagof returned his ticket to the agent. He will arrange to bring his sister and the children here."

Shoushan, Yagof's sister, had managed on her own what Yagof had been unable to accomplish. He visited officials of various agencies, trying vainly to secure permission for his sister to join us. She had fled Mosul to escape vengeful Kurds and had rescued the two boys miraculously. Now she was here. How strange the working of Providence. I had no idea how long it would take for Yagof and Shoushan to get all the red tape unwound for her permission to come to Izmit. So I handled each daily problem as seemed best to me. The people who owned our house asked for permission to use the large second-story hall for the wedding of a relative on the evening of November 12. I saw no reason to deny the request, especially since I had been invited to attend a program at the nearby girls' orphanage that evening. I went off to the orphanage that afternoon, and the wedding party took over our house for their festivities.

After the program I visited briefly with some of the people I knew; then I started toward the front gate. There I met my husband hurrying in. I could hardly believe my eyes. He looked as if he had just escaped from the Death March. His clothes were unkempt, and his face looked drawn and haggard.

"Oh, Marichen!" he exclaimed. "There you are! What is going on, anyhow?" The puzzled expression on his face almost made me laugh despite his obvious bewilderment. "Who are all those people in our house, singing and dancing? Don't we live there anymore?"

"Yagof, dear," I answered, "everything is all right. Those people will be going home as soon as the wedding celebration ends. But you—what has happened to you? You look half dead!"

"For fifteen days I have lived in a tent in this cold weather." Yagof shivered at the thought of the ordeal. "But now Shoushan and the three children are here." He took my arm. "We must get them into the house."

Words simply will not describe the meeting with Yagof's sister. We embraced each other and tears of deep emotion flowed freely. It did not matter to me that she wore shabby garments of widowhood. She was part of Yagof's blood.

Shoushan found her voice first. "Mary dear," she whispered, "I lost five sisters, but I found one just now."

All that night we three adults talked. How could we sleep until we had shared the remarkable providences that had brought us together? Shoushan's story was as full of horror and unbelievable deliverances as was Yagof's or mine.

A day or two later Mother came from Bardezag to help me care for this large addition to my family. I surely needed her kind, patient, gentle, and experienced presence. She brought a few new pieces of furniture the Turkish tenants had been kind enough to leave when they vacated our houses in Bardezag. Besides two almost essential items, a table and a charcoal-burning room heater, she brought corn-husk mattresses, wool comforters, and other items to provide comfortable living.

When Mother returned to Bardezag, she took the two little boys with her so that they could attend the school at the boys' orphanage near her home. Knarig attended school at the girls' orphanage near our home in Izmit. Soon after this I was asked to teach English and Turkish on a part-time basis at the orphanage.

Thus, in relative peace, the year 1919 ran out, ushering in 1920—a year that would bring us to times that would try our souls.

"Confusion and Every Evil Work"

It was in the tumultuous days of 1920 that my sister Varsenig and her husband Onnig Pirenian had to abandon their home in Eskisehir and flee for safety to Bardezag. Heripsime and her family also fled from Shak-shak to join the rest of the family. Yagof and I, with Yagof's sister and her family and Gabriel Pirenian and his family stayed in the old house in Izmit. Thus for a while all our immediate family members were close to each other, and we kept in constant communication. Varsenig and Onnig did not stay long. The conference committee asked them to go to Cilicia, whose chief city is Tarsus, the Apostle Paul's home town, to replace a retiring worker. They went, knowing full well their lives were in jeopardy there.

Our reason for remaining in Izmit, besides the roomy house, was employment. Yagof had a good job at the shoe shop, and both Shoushan and I were on the staff at the girls' orphanage—Shoushan as a seamstress and I as a language teacher.

But Turkish nationalist guerrillas began to close in on Izmit. They surrounded the city, while the British defenders dug trenches and erected sandbag and barbed-wire barricades.

Hostilities broke out one morning with a bombardment of nationalist positions by the big guns on the British warships. One target taking direct hit by explosive shells was a big factory at the head of the bay toward the Bardezag side. From our house we could see the building being reduced to rubble; the action was so close that the bursting bombs shook our house, breaking windows and knocking tiles from the roof.

It soon became obvious that the nationalists still had implacable hatred for Armenians. Several times they tried to set fire to the orphanages in Izmit and in Bardezag, but always their attempts were thwarted by alert watchmen. The British authorities finally served notice that the children should be transported to Istanbul for safety. Sikh troops were sent to Bardezag to cover the evacuation there. Children from both orphanages were hustled aboard a British warship, the *Sardinia*, and staff members were asked to go along. At the time Shoushan and I were both staff members. We had to bid Yagof good-bye. How I wished he could go with us.

"Don't worry, deary," he said. "Maybe I can find a way to go to Istanbul soon and find you."

We both knew that this might be a final separation, but we would not say so. We knew in our hearts that we would be together again in a better land where there will be no war or heartaches.

As the *Sardinia* steamed westward, several times the big guns over our heads opened fire on some target in the hills. The great ship trembled, and the roar almost deafened us. We wondered how the men could stand such conditions day after day.

In Istanbul the orphans and we staff members lived in comfortable quarters provided in a large school complex. Armenian women from the surrounding homes prepared our food in abundance. Except for being separated from my husband and other loved ones, the situation was almost ideal. I actually gained a little weight and felt much better than I had for some time. I knew that I needed to get back to Izmit, but I had no way of going.

One day Yagof and another man surprised me in Istanbul at the orphanage.

"Do you want to come home, deary?" Yagof asked.

"Oh, yes," I said. But in the same breath I asked, "Is it safe?"

"Yes," he assured me. "Fighting has quieted down now. The British have driven off the invaders and have things under control. Oh, the guerrilla fighters are still back in the hills, but they don't bother the city."

We made the necessary arrangements, and I left to go back to Izmit. Shoushan decided to stay a while longer since her three children were in school. We felt soon the whole group would return to Izmit.

Conditions in Izmit were far from ideal. True, no fighting marred the artificial peace; but streams of refugees kept pouring in. Makeshift shelters sprang up around the Armenian church and among the ruined houses near us. Our ever-flowing fountain became the source of supply for more and more families, so many, in fact, that a water shortage developed. Most of these people were in a pitiful condition when they arrived, without sufficient food, clothing, or shelter. Near East Relief gave some meager help as did British governmental agencies, but the volume of abject misery overwhelmed the limited resources available.

Despite the unpleasant situation in Izmit, the orphans were returned from Istanbul not too long after I came home. But the boys could not go back to Bardezag; that campus was still controlled by nationalists. Just down the hill, on the other side of Mother's home, Greek officers occupied our other four houses;

and Mother was in constant danger of being caught by cross fire. She refused to leave, however, because, as she pointed out, we were not much better off in Izmit. Besides, the nationalist soldiers assured her and the few other remaining Armenian residents that there was no danger. They even gave the residents some supplies of food, bedding, and other things— obviously taken from the orphanage storerooms.

Perhaps there was no intended danger, but anyone going between Izmit and Bardezag had to take back roads and sneak through creek beds and crouch behind hedgerows to escape snipers' bullets.

Naturally, human passion, inflamed by injustice and privation, broke out in deeds of violence. Hotheaded Armenians sought for opportunities to get revenge on Turkish nationalists. Many times bands of these Armenian youth infiltrated Turkish areas and returned with trophies of their vengence—plundered Turkish weapons, sacks full of ears cut from slain Turks, or other gruesome items. They boasted of their deeds and expected to receive praise from their countrymen. Of course similar atrocities had been performed by the Turks on fleeing Armenians; but does returning evil for evil bring peace? Our Lord taught His people to love their enemies and do good to those who persecute. But the human heart is slow to learn the ways of righteousness.

Ominous clouds loomed on every side in the early part of 1921. It seemed that at any moment the storm would break, unleashing the fury of demons on the masses of helpless humanity huddled on the shores of beautiful Izmit Bay.

The Storm Breaks

On a Friday afternoon in July 1921 I sat by my large upstairs window overlooking the bay, and Azniv Pirenian came up and sat beside me. There had been an unusually persistent rattle of rifle fire, and we tried to see what was going on. I knew I should be getting ready for the Sabbath, but a presentiment of something dreadful glued me to my seat.

Suddenly the big guns on the bay came alive, and the deafening roar struck terror to our hearts. Almost simultaneously fires broke out in the villages all round the bay. Apparently the nationalists were torching the villages to drive out the inhabitants. We counted seven villages in flames on both sides of Bardezag, including the ancient Greek section of Nicomedia on our side of the bay, but Bardezag remained dark. We wondered if Greek soldiers had held the attackers there because of the Greek officers who lived in our houses. I could not tear myself away from that window even as the night wore on. What would happen to Mother and Heripsime and the children? In agony I prayed for their lives. Thus I spent the whole night.

Later on I learned what happened.

Early in the morning Greek officers had ordered everyone to evacuate Bardezag and go to the beaches.

During the night hundreds of refugees had scurried down ravines and creek beds toward the bay with whatever they could carry. Some of the hill dwellers had driven their cows ahead of them. Large numbers of wounded Greek soldiers awaited rescue ships. The beaches were crowded by masses of confused human beings and clusters of lowing cows.

Heripsime and her children went down to the beach with the Shak-shak people. Naomi, Heripsime's oldest daughter, had married a Shak-shak boy shortly after the return from Konya. When they reached the beach, they began to look for our Mother.

Mother had prepared a large bundle of things she considered essential. She managed to half drag, half carry the bundle out to the road, but she couldn't get anyone to help her to the beach. Everyone was too concerned with personal affairs. She hesitated. Should she abandon the bundle, or should she try to find someone to take it to Izmit? (I don't know how she thought anyone could get through to Izmit.) So she waited. Then she saw John-boy, Heripsime's son, now a husky teenager, riding up the hill on a horse. He had felt he could not leave his beloved grandmother, so he had borrowed a horse and come back to look for her, risking his own life. When he found her, she had almost decided to abandon the bundle.

What a scene of confusion Mother found on the seashore. Desperate people crowded into all kinds of boats, trying to reach safety on the big ships. Bundles and people fell into the water in the desperate struggle for passage. Farmers drove their cows and horses into the water and then tried to make them swim across to Izmit. Others tied the animals to sailboats and then tried to tow them across. Dead and wounded soldiers lay in long rows until someone could carry them to boats. And all the while the big guns and screaming shells made such a din that one could hardly hear anyone else. Amid all this confusion Mother and her loved ones managed to stay together. They found themselves on a big Greek ship headed for safety.

Back in Izmit I could see the activity across the bay, but it was too far away for me to know exactly what was happening.

On Sabbath morning a young man from the shoeshop came to our house. Mother had somehow managed to find someone who could get through to Izmit with a note to tell us about her leaving Bardezag with the Greeks. Yagof immediately went with the young man, intending to bring Mother and the others to Izmit. They found a small boat and started to cross the bay, but military authorities turned them back. It would take less than an hour to row across to Bardezag, but they argued in vain for permission. So near, and yet so far. All we could learn was that the people on the big ships would be taken to friendly Greek islands, possibly even to the mainland. They would be safe, we were assured.

About a week later we were told that Izmit would also be evacuated. Conditions in the city deteriorated rapidly. Refugees on the outskirts moved into the city with their farm animals. Soon stray cattle roamed the streets, and hungry people slaughtered many of them for meat. Fighting between annoyed Turkish residents and vengeful refugees broke out in the marketplaces and public plazas. Confusion reigned, and tensions mounted. The British managed to keep the railroad open to Uskudar (Scutari) across from Istanbul, and every outgoing train carried a capacity load.

Many of us tried to remain calm. We did not want to be the first to run away. Maybe the crisis would pass again, and we would be allowed to stay in our comfortable houses.

In the middle of August, nearly three weeks after the evacuation of Bardezag, word came that we must prepare to leave. People crowded down to the beaches. Still we lingered. I will never forget the last two nights in that lonely house.

In order to avoid stray bullets we put our mattresses on the floor in the big central hall upstairs and slept with our clothes on so that we would not have to dress in case of an emergency. We could not have any light in the house, knowing that trigger-happy snipers would welcome a target. In order to have worship before retiring we gathered in a back room on the ground floor where light from a small candle would not be seen outside. There we huddled solemnly while Gabriel read a few verses of Scripture and we all joined in prayer for safety.

On the morning of the second day Gabriel's little daughter Esther came running up the hill from the orphanage where she had gone for the day at school. Miss Holt, the director, sent me a message urging me to join her and other staff members there. She felt sure that the orphanage would be protected. "Don't stay another night in that dangerous place," she implored. "You will be safe here."

"Only an insane person would stay in this house longer," said Gabriel. "We must take what we can carry and get down to the beach."

I tried to remain calm as I gathered a few essential things and made up a bundle for Yagof to carry. I carried a jug of water, a lantern, and a few other items.

We went to the orphanage first to talk with Miss Holt and Yagof's sister Shoushan. Again Miss Holt tried to persuade me to stay with her. Shoushan and her daughter Knarig were staying there.

I could not bring myself to seek my own safety and watch Yagof go off to some unknown place. I could not forget all the heartaches caused by separations in the exile less than six years before. I would not risk losing this man to whom my life was firmly bound. With a heavy heart I walked down to the beach with Yagof and Kegam, Gabriel and his children, and a few other friends. We spread bedding on the sand and tried to rest. It seemed that we would have to spend the night there.

Suddenly through the darkness a strong voice sounded above the hubbub. "People, hurry!" the voice boomed out in the Armenian tongue. "This is the last boat. Let no one remain on shore!"

Could we believe it? Yes, it was the voice of Patriarch Stephanos, head of the Armenian Church for the whole province. He would not lie. We all knew him as a faithful shepherd.

"This is the very last boat!" the voice had an impelling urgency. "Let no one remain out there!"

We scrambled to our feet and hurriedly gathered up our belongings. Yagof and Kegam worked in a frenzy to throw things into the boat. With my water jug and lantern, and holding two of the children by the hands, I struggled toward the pier competing with Greek soldiers for space. A searchlight from a nearby warship shone on the pier to provide illumination.

The bright light blinded my eyes, and I stumbled on a wooden cleat on the pier. Down I went on my elbows and knees. An officer on the ship saw me fall, and he ran to help me. He lifted me to my feet and led me up the narrow gangplank to the deck. Friendly Armenians on board helped me find a place to sit. Soon Yagof and Gabriel and the boys came aboard, soaked with perspiration, and sank exhausted among the baggage. They had succeeded in getting aboard all but a good folding bed and one trunk. It was three o'clock in the morning.

Later Shoushan told us she tried to go to the beach early that morning to see if she could find out about us, but soldiers turned her away. She learned that the few who had remained ashore were found dead when daylight came.

Now aboard the Greek ship my loved ones and friends turned their attention to me. They were all concerned because of my condition—seven months pregnant. You see, before this I had already had several miscarriages. My physical condition and several traumatic experiences since our marriage had caused me to lose previous unborn children in the early weeks and months. This time I had pleaded with the Lord to let me bear a son. Yagof, one of a family of twelve, wanted a child very much. Now we all hoped that I could carry this one to full term. A friend of Yagof's, one of Patriarch Stephanos's aides, who was on shipboard, found me a place to lie down in a room below the deck. Two other friends who managed to be on board went with me.

The ship carrying us away from danger had been rented with money raised by Armenian orphans in Istanbul. Those dear children volunteered to live on olives and bread for several days so that money usually spent for other food could be used to save the lives of people they did not even know.

When we boarded the ship, we had no idea where it would take us. The ship steamed out of the bay of Izmit and headed out across the Sea of Marmara. Then we learned that Patriarch Stephanos would try to land us at the Greek town of Rodosto which is now called Tekirdag on the northwest shore of that sea rather than heading for Greek islands in the Aegean.

Late that same evening our ship anchored at Rodosto. Again Yagof, Gabriel, and the boys worked to the point of exhaustion to get our things together on the pier. They spread out some bedding at last, and we all lay down to rest as best we could until morning.

With the dawn people from the town—refugees from previous shiploads—came down to the pier to find out if any of their loved ones or friends might be among the new arrivals. What was our amazment to see a familiar form limping along—my dear mother. Her sister was with her. What a happy reunion. We had no idea that these dear ones had come to this haven. And Mother told us that Heripsime and her people were there also. We learned that several Adventist families had found refuge in this friendly town.

We found a large, three-story house having a large room on each of the first two floors and a small attic room on the third. Gabriel and his family occupied the first floor; Yagof, his brother Kegam, and I had the middle floor; and some of the children slept in the attic room.

More or less settled in new living quarters, I hoped for a chance to rest and build up my strength. Of course I would have to take care of normal household duties, but surely, I thought, those would be light.

Elder Erzberger, having learned that quite a number of Adventists had congregated in Rodosto, came from Istanbul to encourage the members. And since our house offered the best place for him to stay, and since I was his translator, he stayed with us.

I was happy to be able to help in the Lord's work, but my physical condition was not strong. Standing on my feet so much during the latter part of my pregnancy did not help my weakened condition.

A New Life

Day after day—week after week—I waited patiently for the arrival of my little one. The expected time passed, and still no labor pains announced the time. The Armenian midwife, a resident of Rodosto, came several times to inquire about the state of affairs. She did not express her fears, but her manner and her questions betrayed her worry.

Finally one morning the pains started. The midwife gave orders for the necessary preparations. My mother, who had moved in with us to care for me, hurried downstairs to heat water, praying earnestly all the while for our loving Father's care.

I did not intend to tell anyone, but soon neighbors and friends began to gather. Everyone was ready—except the unborn child. The pains subsided. The women went away disappointed. Mother allowed the fire to die and returned to her mat.

The following night the same thing happened.

The next day. Another night.

The second night intense labor pains came on.

"Now at this moment, it is coming!" the midwife exclaimed. "It's coming for sure!"

I heard the women by my side whispering. What were they whispering about? Then I heard our landlady say that she had witnessed similar deliveries in Bulgaria, Romania, and other places, but never one just like this. She walked around the room chanting, "Hear us, Lord; hear us. Have mercy on us, Father in heaven."

I later learned that Gabriel, who lived on the floor below us, could not sleep that night. Vivid memories of his own wife's death under the same circumstances plagued his mind. Men of the family were not supposed to interfere in such affairs, but he felt impelled to talk to Yagof.

"This girl is just like my wife, Isguhie," he blurted. "Before the child was born, she died." A sob choked his voice momentarily. "And we lost the baby too."

"What can we do?" Yagof asked weakly. "The midwife is in charge."

"Don't pay any attention to what the midwife says," Gabriel said. "We must go right now and find a physician. This is a matter of life or death. Go at once, Yagof."

Yagof bit his lip uncertainly.

"Listen to me, man!" Gabriel took hold of Yagof's shoulders and peered into his face. "We must try to save her. I can't bear to have another woman lost for lack of proper care. In Konya I could not get a doctor, but there is one here right in our neighborhood. Get the doctor who can save her life."

So the two men dashed off to the house where Dr. Der Stepanian lived. He was out on a case.

They ran to the home of another doctor in another part of town. He already was away.

At both places they left word of the emergency and asked the doctor to come as soon as possible.

Back in the upper room the women continued their efforts to deliver the child. "Just now it will come, dear," the weary midwife cooed. "Hang onto these rings. That's right. Now bear down a little more—just a little more."

I could not bear down any harder. I had no more strength. Mother hobbled up and down the stairs time and again. Over and over she went to a little room and sank to her knees in earnest prayer for my life.

At last a little after midnight a vigorous knock sounded on the outside door. Someone opened the door, and Dr. Der Stepanian bounded up the stairs, panting from the exertion and with his satchel in hand. He strode across the room to the *sedirlik* where I had lain for three days, felt my pulse, and patted my forhead with a compassionate touch. Then he left the room. He beckoned for Mother to follow him. I heard him call for Yagof to come upstairs. Silence reigned; the chattering women now stood around apprehensively.

I could hear snatches of a consultation just outside the partly closed door. The doctor's voice carried better than the others. "Only a few minutes left—" "If the husband permits—" "Hope we can deliver her from death—" "All right, then." The voice indicated that the doctor had entered the room. "I have your permission; I will proceed."

The doctor politely made his way through the cluster of women at my bedside—seven of them—and placed his satchel on the floor. He opened the satchel and laid out the shining instruments on a clean towel. He motioned for two of the women to assist him, and then he went to work.

My life and the life of the unborn child rested in the hands of this skillful doctor—and in the tender care of the Great Physician.

Soon the doctor stood up with a crumpled and bruised infant in his hands. "Take this away," he said to one of the women. Obviously he did not think the child would live. At the moment he had the task of saving my life. Because of a shortage of medical supplies, the doctor had to work on me without benefit of anesthetic of any kind. I simply had to grit my teeth and bear the pain as he quickly sewed up the torn tissues. The repairs completed, he tied my knees together with a strip of cloth and gave orders that I must lie on my back for three weeks. Gentle hands lifted my head and shoulders and placed soft pillows to elevate that part of my body, and I settled back for rest—peaceful rest.

Meanwhile the women had done the necessary work of caring for the baby and cleaning up the room. The doctor, now satisfied that I would survive, went to the other end of the *sedirlik* and picked up the bundle to see what he had delivered. He found a healthy infant breathing normally and looking very much alive. "This child must weigh fourteen pounds!" the doctor marveled. "He looks as if he is already three months old." He shook his head in disbelief. "No wonder the poor mother had such a difficult time." He left the room shaking his head.

About six weeks later after Baby John arrived I began to notice hardness and swelling in my left breast. The midwife and other well-meaning women suggested various home treatments, and Mother faithfully tried them all—fomentations and poultices of various kinds.

For two weeks I endured increasing pain. Baby John refused to nurse from that side, and he would not take a bottle. Mother did manage to get him to take a little milk or water from a spoon.

Finally the pain became so unbearable that I sat up in bed all one night. The next morning Dr. Der Stephanian made an appointment for me at the military hospital about three miles out of town. How would we get to the hospital? We could not afford to hire a carriage; the only other alternative was to walk. So, with Heripsime and Shoushan to help me, I walked. It was a bitterly cold day in the dead of winter, and my heavy shawl was hardly enough to keep me warm. Enduring excruciating pain and almost fainting several times, I kept plodding on until we reached the hospital. It seemed an endless journey.

Then we couldn't find a place to sit down. We entered a huge room crowded with wounded, dying, and some dead soldiers. A doctor finally opened a door at one side and motioned us to come. We picked our way across the room, stepping carefully around the men lying on the floor. At the door he firmly told my aunt and my sister to wait outside.

"Let me see what you have, young lady," the doctor said. Then, when he saw the swelling and the angry blue-green color of that infected breast, his face registered disbelief. "It is the very last minute!" he breathed. "This would have developed into gangrene if you had not come at this moment." He almost shoved me toward the table. "Get up on the table and lie on your back, clasping your hands over your head." He plucked a knife from the jar of antiseptic solution. "Now don't move!" Then, without any kind of pain killer, he lanced the breast as if he were cutting a melon. A nurse standing beside the table held a basin to catch the foul-smelling discharge.

The whole operation happened so fast that I hardly had time to scream, and the instant relief from the pressure and pain left me almost breathless. What a relief!

The doctor bandaged the gaping hole. "Change the bandage several times a day," he ordered.

Shortly after the ordeal I began my walk back home

with the aid once more of Heripsime and Shoushan, who supported me and urged me on. Weakness and pain overcame me several times. Once at home I took to my bed on the *sedirlik* and fell into a deep sleep. Mother brought me hot food, but all I wanted to do was sleep. Gradually I gained my strength back. But for a long time I had recurring attacks of swelling of the breast and fever.

During that winter of 1921 and 1922 the rumor mill worked as usual. This Greek town of Rodosto was in Turkish territory that the Allies intended to hand over to Greece. The increasing success of the nationalists in Anatolia caused concern that this area might also come under attack. So exiles began trying to move to safer places.

Because of Yagof 's Russian citzenship, we could not go into Greece or any of the neighboring Balkan countries. Again, as before in Konya, we decided that our best option would be to return to Istanbul. Yagof would go first and get work as a shoemaker.

Yagof had little trouble getting permission for himself, and he left us with the trust that God would take care of us. Neither he nor I imagined that three long months would drag by before we could wheedle the necessary papers from reluctant authorities.

Finally the day came when we were ready to leave for Istanbul. Although we did not know it at the time, this parting marked the breakup of my close-knit family. Heripsime's daughter, Naomi, had already gone to Greece with the Shak-shak people, and her older son John had gone to Argentina. Heripsime and her two younger children stayed in Rodosto for a while longer, and then they also went to Greece and later on to Argentina. Varsenig and her husband, Onnig, who had gone to Cilicia, met with persecution and had to flee the country. Onnig died of a fever and exhaustion, and my sister Varsenig went to Greece. We never saw any of them again.

Mother and I, and baby John and Yagof's brother Kegam, boarded a ship for Istanbul. What the future held for us we could only guess. We hoped that our days of pilgrimage were at an end. Could we finally settle down in peace?

Land of Promise

Life in Istanbul fell into an easy routine. Shoushan and the two children, Knarig and Levon, who had remained in the orphanage at Izmit, joined us in a lovely home Yagof rented for us. To all appearances every thing was in our favor. But an uneasy apprehension brooded over the city. A dread of Mustafa Kemal's possible attitude towards Armenians caused our people to seek safety in other countries. We hesitated. Where should we go? The same old ghost haunted us—Yagof's Russian citizenship. That citizenship had proved a blessing to us over and over; but it had also narrowed our choices of asylum.

Many Armenian families wanted to go to the United States of America. Letters from friends already there described unbelievably ideal conditions. Many of these letters came from the farming country around Fresno, California, located in the rich San Joaquin Valley. But over and over we heard it said, "It's easier to enter the kingdom of heaven than America."

One day Yagof came home from work more upset than usual. "Why don't we wake up and get out of this place while we can?" he blurted.

"How about going to the U.S.A.?" he asked one day.

"There isn't a chance," I countered.

"Let me find out," he said. And we retired for the night to dream of the life in the "land of the free" far to the west.

Yagof bounded into the house the next afternoon. "The U.S.A. has a large quota for Russians!" he announced. "Oh, Marichen! Let's get your sisters to come here and join us, and we'll all go to America."

"Yagof," I said as calmly as possible, "don't forget that they are not Russian subjects. We'll be most fortunate if we succeed in getting permission for your sister and Knarig, your two brothers, my mother, Baby John and me, and you—that's eight people with only one wage earner, and you are twenty-seven-years old!"

On Tuesday, November 28, 1922, Yagof (now using the English form of the name Jacob) started work in earnest to secure proper passports with visas for eight of us to enter the United States. Standing in line. Interviews. Questionnaires. Testimonials. Witnessess. Financial checks. Around and around we went from one office to another. With American officials Jacob couldn't speak English. With Russian officials I couldn't speak Russian. One thing we would not do: We would not bribe in hopes of speeding up the process. We had learned a lesson on that.

Finally in January 1923 we received our visas— all eight of them. Then we began in earnest getting ready for the most daring venture of our lives. We worked hard and saved money. Jacob did shoemaking and leather work for U.S. Navy officers on an American cruiser in the habor.

By June we were ready to go. Final papers, medical certificates, and all other arrangements had been completed. We had booking aboard the U.S.S. *Canada* for June 12, 1923.

One night before our departure we met with friends

and relatives for a farewell dinner. Such a sad-happy occasion. The dear ones with whom our lives had been entwined would now be left behind; we were embarking on an adventure with unknown consequences. But we spent time encouraging one another and sharing hopes for a brighter tomorrow—if not in this life, at least in God's bright new world when Jesus comes.

One feature of that dinner stands out in my mind, Sister Agavnie Armenag Papazian had prepared a huge pan of delicious böreg—a very sweet kind of squash (honey squash) rolled in batter. Sister Papazian was an expert with that particular dish.

Tuesday morning our little group of eight walked up the gangplank carrying all our earthly goods in six suitcases. Mother carried Baby John. Then we stood on the deck and waved to our loved ones below as tears dampened our cheeks and big lumps in our throats threatened to choke us. Tugs nudged our ship away from the dock and out toward the channel. Soon we were gliding down the Bosporus toward the Sea of Marmara, and the waving hands of our friends faded in the distance.

As the ship plowed toward the setting sun that evening, a strange sense of unreality settled over us. Could it be possible that we were leaving behind us the intense racial religious biases that had plagued our lives and decimated our nation? Would we really find peace at last in "the land of the free"?

The voyage through the Mediterranean gave us several glorious days and star-spangled nights. A stop at Naples with Vesuvius towering behind the city offered opportunity for tourists to visit Pompeii or climb the volcano. We did not have money for such luxuries.

Soon after we sailed through the storied Pillars of Hercules (Strait of Gibraltar), we knew we had entered the stormy Atlantic. The ocean lived up to its reputation by giving us, not a stormy night, but a constant storm for the full twelve days of crossing. Everyone on board except the most seasoned travelers succumbed to the infamous mal de mer. I thought I would die.

The most traumatic part of the whole trip, however, was the ordeal on Ellis Island. U.S. immigration officers were kind, but particular to a fault. First we couldn't convince them that Mother had a right to be with us. Then we tried to get permission for temporary residence in New York so that Jacob could earn money for fare to California. This went on for days. We thought for sure we would be sent back to Turkey. Telegrams crackled to Jacob's uncle in Fresno, a Mr. Torosian, and answers came back. Finally, after twelve days of desperation, our relatives in California had to get together enough money to get us to California, and then the officials cleared us to leave our "prison."

The bountiful orchards and vineyards of California's San Joaquin Valley became to us literally the "land of promise." We arrived there just in time for the apricot harvest. Then came peaches and after that grapes.

What a wonderful country! Flowing with milk and honey! And freedom! We knew we were safe at last.

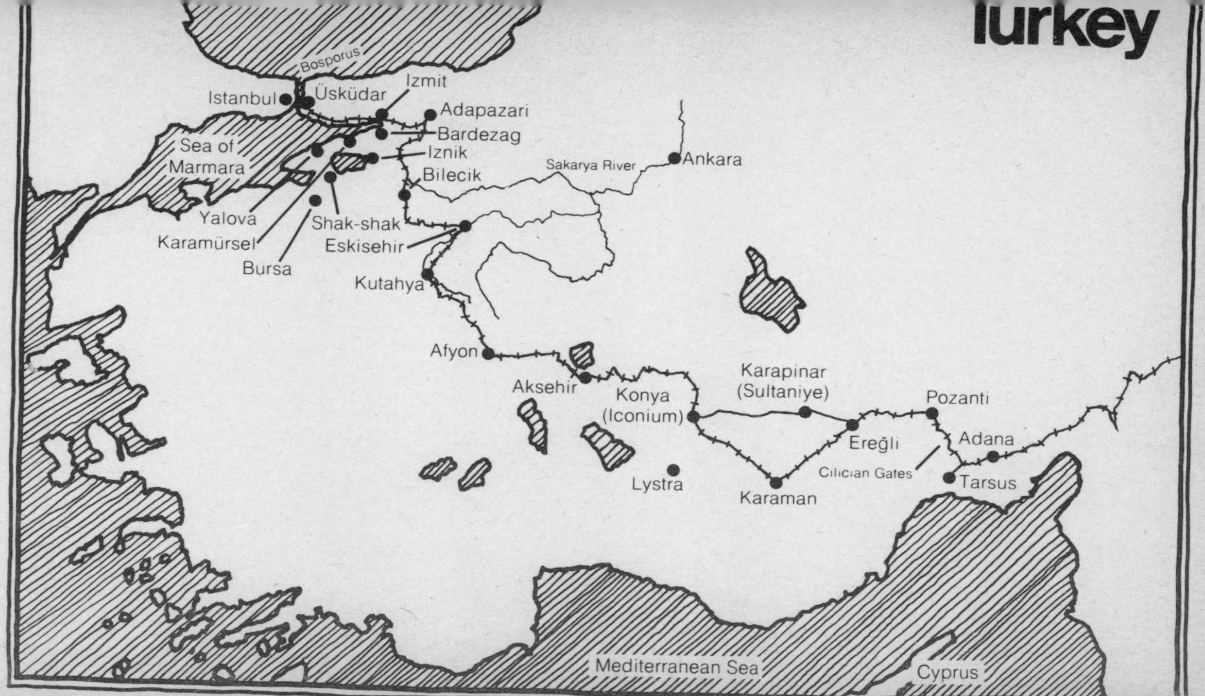

Turkey

Bosporus
Istanbul
Üsküdar
Izmit
Adapazari
Bardezag
Iznik
Bilecik
Sea of
Marmara
Yalova
Karamürsel
Bursa
Shak-shak
Eskisehir
Kutahya
Sakarya River
Ankara
Afyon
Aksehir
Konya
(Iconium)
Karapinar
(Sultaniye)
Lystra
Karaman
Ereğli
Cilician Gates
Pozanti
Adana
Tarsus
Mediterranean Sea
Cyprus

Marie had this picture taken in Turkey. This is the picture Yagof finally received from his beloved Marie before their marriage.

Yagof and Marie shortly after their wedding late in 1917.

Yagof and Marie Egitkhanoff with their four children and Marie's mother, seated, some time after arriving in California.